ALL RIGHT SO FAR

Also by Sheila Balls

Somebody Move the Cat!
Our Side of the Fence

All Right So Far

Finding our way in the Not-So-Deep Woods

Sheila Balls

Moo Alley Press

All Right So Far

Finding our way in the Not-So-Deep Woods

Copyright © 2018 by Sheila Balls

All rights reserved. This book or any portion thereof may not be reproduced or used in any manner whatsoever without the express written permission of the publisher except for the use of brief quotations in a book review.

Paperback Edition ISBN: 978-1-7751185-0-3

Kindle Direct Publishing Edition

mooalleypress.ca

Moo Alley Press

278 Graham St, Unit 17
Meaford, Ontario N4L 1Y3

Cover Artwork: Suzanne Wakefield   Book Design: Tim Reilly
Art Integration: Eva Smith   Illustrations: Stuart Robertson

Preface and Acknowledgements

Towards morning but still fully dark I am wakened by the soft pad of a cat stepping carefully across the bed to look into my face: "Are you awake?"

I used to write then, up at the lake, those nights I could not sleep, but it has been a long time since I felt like writing through the dark hours ... maybe because of the 'dark hours' we have gone through in our own life.

In those years we lived in The Not-So-Deep-Woods, my husband and I navigated our way through a faltering marriage and health conditions hard to imagine unless you are the one living them. Thank heavens we could not see ahead, to know how much scarier the journey would get, how much loss we as a couple, and especially Carl, would face.

Still, the darkness of loss lets you see more clearly that there is light too, the light of friends and family and happy times, the understanding that if you hold hands and move forward you can in the end be all right.

This book has been simmering for a number of years. In that time family, friends, and other writers have listened, shared and steered me towards its completion. I am grateful to all of them and to Suzanne Wakefield for the cover painting, Eva Smith for final art assembly, and Stuart Robertson for his illustrations. My children Michael and Catherine contributed in many ways, and a team of advance readers offered good advice. I owe an especially big thank you to Tim Reilly for the interior design plus his many months of guidance and encouragement.

For Carl, who so often echoed the words of
Disney's Thumper the rabbit,

"Some fun huh, Bambi?"

I have known this little poem most of my life. Telling myself, *I am all right so far* has helped me through a disintegrating marriage and my husband's dramatic health journey.

*The optimist fell ten stories
and at each window bar,
He called to his friends
who watched from above:
"All right so far!"*

The Not So Deep Woods

Contents

Headed Downhill

Health Train, Marriage Train...3
Being Plaid..8
A 'V' and an 'X'...11
Present Friend, Absent Husband..13
Take This Job, or..16
Soul Neglected (Carl Sleeps)...19
Is It All Right?...23
The Remedy for Suffering..27
"While You're Making Other Plans"..31
Riding the Coaster...36
It's Not Brain Surgery... Or Is It?...38
This Is the One...41
This Is Your Brain...43
Traditions...46
Last Leg of the Journey...50
Ready to Bargain...52
Dancing in the Dark..56
Candles in the Window..59
Breathing Room..62
Fragments and Remnants..66
Lessons...69
The Inner Child is Out..73
Solace...78

Getting Back on Track

Bad Memories, Good Dreams..85
Exploring a Marriage...89
Wedding Bells...93
On Retreat..97
Issues..100
Life is Only...105
'C' Stands For 108
Give Me Strength!...111

Messages	115
Sex and Violence	117
Broken Places	119
Long Winter	123
Taming the Bear	126
Encounters	130
Expecting	133
Operation	135

New Directions

The Entertainment	141
Signs	143
A Little Drama Here and There	147
One Cow Running	151
Sheila vs The Hill	155
Fast Food	157
Are We There Yet?	159
Birdwatchers	164
Nature Calling	166
Comfort Objects	170
Emergency	173
Hospital	178
Happy Anniversary	182
Date Night, Medical Style	185
'Normal' is a Relative Term	189
Alarm	192
Panini Generation	194
Appearances	199
Three Minute Mission	202
Have I Got the House For You!	204
Packing it Up	208
Katie's Purse	212
Essential Services and Peaceful Places	216
Letter to Carl	218
Calendar	219
Epilogue	223
About the Author	225

Part I

Headed Downhill

Health Train, Marriage Train

Twenty years now I have watched treacherous infection in close company with the diagnosis of a rare and frightening neurological disorder, whittle away at the heart of my husband, lover and friend, pushing us as a couple into being people we had never been before. For a while our marriage began to collapse around us. Perhaps that's how we two optimists fell over the edge and out of our previously comfortable life in the first place.

Nobody's life is perfect, but ours was good. We were friends first and foremost, Carl strong of body, quick of wit, dynamic and fun loving. Me, reflective in nature and somewhat inexperienced in how the world worked. There was much to celebrate in our marriage. We supported one another by filling in the gaps. Where I was a planner, calendars and lists in hand to keep me on the straight and narrow, Carl was more spontaneous, a hands-on person. With hammer and drill, he tackled household projects fearlessly, stopping only occasionally to look at the appropriate instruction sheet. I organized family events and felt privileged that my husband trusted me to make most of the big decisions.

We designed and built three houses in the years we raised our children. There was one unwritten rule: you had to be able to walk to or see water. Our life usually included a stray cat to adopt, and a garden to tend, a choir to sing with, a figure skating or black light theater show to produce. I could sit contentedly in a corner with a book, but the man I married needed to be *out there* creating, whether it was with a spoon, a rake, or a paintbrush.

Life was good to us and I knew it. Somewhere inside I believed that if I never took that for granted, if I was appropriately grateful, then things would stay the same. But things never stay the same. Lives can alter in an instant. With us the changes slipped up from behind like waves piling the water higher and higher. Crisis followed crisis until we grew used to ambulances hurtling through the forest, taxis delivering medications, and nurses bustling in and out of our home.

Over the years I would learn to keep my meds and toiletries packed in a little bag ready to grab at a moment's notice. In time I would become skilled at predicting which entrances ambulance attendants would use and where to shove furniture in order to create pathways for a stretcher. The dining room table stood on little rolling casters so it could be moved out of the way in a hurry. Friends kept copies of our emergency contact list and my wallet always held change for hospital parking lots.

The way we lived and even the way we had always seen ourselves was about to disappear, leaving us newly born into a baffling world where some friends surrounded us while others drew back, where discussions had to go straight to the heart of the matter without the customary subtleties. It projected us into a world where tiny familiarities took on new importance as we struggled to inject some feeling of *normal* into our days.

Hand in hand with the medical situation, came the fading out of a previously vibrant marriage, one partner not even noticing, the other bewildered at first, then increasingly anxious to restore the way it used to be. It felt like we were thundering along on twin trains of health and marriage crisis, with no one at the controls. It felt like life sped up just when it was supposed to slow down.

For several years Carl's balance had deteriorated. Walking wasn't as automatic as it used to be or should be. Legs which once carried him over the waves on water skis now lacked strength. As early as eight years ago we had recognized that something neurological was going on, but several months and many tests later, doctors could only agree on what it wasn't. It wasn't MS. And if it wasn't MS, then nobody seemed to know what to do.

Seasons passed as they always had. Except that in those days of push lawnmowers, cutting half an acre of lawns at The North Acre, as we called our property, now required all four of us working twice a week, and the children were about to finish high school and leave home. I had taken Carl's considerable physical strength for granted.

At times when I played dinner music for banquets it had been commonplace to see him stagger up the basement stairs arms wrapped around a sizeable electric organ which leaned against his chest. Increasingly now, he appeared troubled by simple tasks like gardening: "My legs feel as if I have just run a race," he told me.

It would be two decades before anyone would understand the significance of those words.

It was time to look at our situation with new eyes. I began to consider the house I had designed especially for our family's needs, right down to a laundry chute placed directly above the washing machine. Of the twenty-seven windows, all but three faced south, placed that way to draw the heat. "This has always been my favourite room," my friend Dianne said, pointing towards bedroom windows with a view of Georgian Bay and Owen Sound off to the south.

Upon opening a French door, you stepped down into a sun porch where our beloved little cat Nick, black and silken haired, beautiful but weak of heart, had retreated towards the end of his life. His eyes were fixed in my memory, apologizing: "I can't get downstairs anymore. I'm sick. Can you bring my litter box up here?" Even the sad memories held me in this house.

At the center of the living area, one or another of us would stand by a big roll top desk rescued years earlier from the farm where Carl grew up. The waist high wall backing the living room had been hollowed out to hold plants. I knew if we left this house we would miss seeing that planter filled with Christmas poinsettias.

I continued to bake cookies in the identical copy of our previous kitchen (when you find something you like, stick with it). Directly beneath this area was our son Michael's bedroom. Here we had installed industrial strength carpet in deference to his fondness for science experiments. Who would put electrodes in a pot of earth? And why?

The window in our daughter Catherine's room had white curtains and a window blind her father had painted with a design of pink flowers. Carl was a father who created little touches to make his children feel special. He carpentered, he sewed, he painted, he glued. Just outside, he and Michael had built a soapbox racer in the driveway. But nobody was building soapbox racers now. Michael was off to school and his sister only seventeen months younger. We were edging towards being two people in a too-big house with a high maintenance yard.

Was it time to move on? Often in the evening I walked round and round the perimeter of the yard thinking, "Can we give this up ... the gardens Carl has spent years preparing? The little hand-dug fishpond where raccoons come to drink?" But my husband's strength was clearly waning, I came to the decision that *giving something up* was not a helpful way of looking at our situation. Think instead about what we would be moving towards.

Thankfully the decision to move became our choice rather than change forced upon us through health concerns. For a long while Carl showed no further neurological symptoms. His legs did not get any better, but neither did they get any worse.

When Catherine started university, we acquired a new kitten. All our previous pets had been strays old enough to find their way to our homes. This was our first experience with a baby animal small enough to curl up in the soup bowl we expected her to drink from. Abby was a dainty white and tabby longhaired creature who soon learned to creep under the covers of the bed if she was cold.

"You replaced me with a kitten?" Catherine protested.

Kitten or not, the house was quieter with the children gone. We had lived there for our kids' growing up years but now we wondered if a smaller place might do. On quiet Sunday afternoons we often drove out to Bass Lake to see if any properties had come up for sale. When a small cottage not even half the size of our present house had come on the market, we looked at it and dismissed the tiny kitchen as unlikely to work for us. But it was not easy to buy a property on Bass Lake. Should we re-think this situation? At under a thousand square feet, the cottage was well within our budget. Perhaps we could afford to add to it, bringing it to a more comfortable size if we did it in stages.

 To this point we had always had the luxury of designing our own homes. Once when I complained of not feeling confident, Carl said to me: "You draw a house on a piece of paper and hand it to a builder and say 'Build this.' What's not confident about that?"

We turned for advice, as we had done before, to builder Elgin Rouse. He emerged from beneath the Bass Lake cottage to stand in the frigid living room facing our real estate agent. "There is a beam which needs replacing," Elgin began. We wanted to hear his opinions, but were all distracted by the cold. Elgin showed us how to stand on one leg and swing the other back and forth, an old trick, he said, used by guys who have to work outside. "It will keep your feet a bit warmer." Beneath the house, he explained, the temperature was actually warmer than here inside it. "The house is built on rock and it holds the heat."

Overall, it seemed the place was in good shape. We had always heard that 'the day you buy a house is the day you sell it.' We felt reassured that we were doing the right thing.

Immediately the roof would need replacing, and in the woods steel roofs though expensive are needed, as evidenced by the moss collecting on the current roof. In the beginning we could heat almost entirely with a wood stove supplemented by a few electric baseboard heaters. Carl had lived to age twelve without indoor plumbing. Heating with a woodstove did not seem such a burden to him.

We could afford a small addition but the floor of this new bedroom would be plywood covered with a coat of paint. Our niece would later describe the room as 'charming', and I loved her for that comment. But 'primitive' might be more accurate. Still it had everything we really needed and the cottage would make a comfortable home, comparatively easy to care for after the larger place at the North Acre.

From the front of the house a clearing offered a view of sunrise over the lake. Behind the house the forest gave way to a sunny meadow where the neighbour's cattle grazed. Best of all, where yard care had formerly involved lawnmowers and plenty of them, we would now need chainsaws and the telephone number of a good arborist. Lawn Care was about to be replaced by Forest Management.

Being Plaid

I HAD REASONED THAT APRIL WOULD be a good month for moving, all danger of winter being past. What was I thinking? *Am I not Canadian? Do I not know that winter likes one last kick at the can late in the season?* A nine hundred square foot cottage now bulging with the contents of a twenty-four hundred square foot house, certainly has no room for two dozen plants, so we lost quite a few as they sat tarp-covered in the yard.

That first night at the lake a late winter storm blew in, coating the trees with ice. The following day, wherever you walked outdoors you could hear tiny remnants of ice playing a crystal song by striking one another as they fell from the trees. Urged along by the wild wind, great pans of ice sailed down the lake at high speed. I was enthralled, thinking we would hear the crystal music and see the ice pans fly past every spring, but this turned out to be a once in a lifetime experience.

An experience I would not enjoy was navigating the bush road from the house to the highway. The roads met at the top of a hill. Not a high hill, but high enough for a car to drift backwards and turn sideways blocking neighbours from going up or down. Near the foot of the hill, a curve made both directions invisible to one another. Approaching from the bottom you dare not get up speed until you were sure nobody was coming down the hill, and if the surface happened to be slippery it took a certain amount of momentum to carry you safely to the top.

Carl never worried about the hill. He loved coming home at the end of his workday, no matter the season. "I just feel the tension let go when I leave the highway for that last two minute drive to the house," he said. I did not share his sentiments. I wished we could travel together but our working hours differed too much. Sighing with relief as I emerged onto the highway on winter days, I saw the hill as an obstacle to be faced and conquered. How far away was spring? "Only eighty-four (or sixty-two or forty-eight) more times to do this," I would think, gripping the steering wheel with mittened hands.

For me, facing that stretch of road in winter was the only negative part of going to school each day. I knew very young I would be a teacher. There was a week or so in there at age seven, when I thought being a clown would be fun, but when Jimmy M. took me to his basement after school and introduced me to his dog 'Prince of the Black Hedges', and showed me the school desks where we could play school (even though we had just come from the real thing) somewhere in the back of my mind, I knew.

The fact that there was a teachers' college right in town helped. My Mom, widowed for four years, could not have afforded post-secondary education for me otherwise. And the bursary I won helped too. It bought me a beautiful warm coat for walking to school in the cold winter.

Teachers' college let me feel at home in a way I had never experienced in high school. I felt the same way I had those past three summers on staff at a day camp. And the common denominator? Children of course! I liked being with them. I liked encouraging them and showing them new things, whether on a nature walk pointing out the sound of a Canada jay, or sitting at a desk planning a class project. There is a *right here/right now* feeling in being with a child which most adults have lost somewhere along the line. Children are impatient, but maybe it is because they have so much to learn, they just can't wait to get started.

We had fully expected when we moved, to teach four or five more years. The Grey County Board of Education at that time operated on a *ninety factor* decreeing that you could retire when your current age, added to the number of years you had been working, totaled ninety. Carl, having entered grade one in his community's little one room school house at age four, had started teaching at eighteen. Still, ninety had always seemed far in the distance. Then suddenly, with the spring, came the news: the ninety factor had been backed up to eighty. The early retirement window opened and we jumped out, Carl joyfully, and I more introspectively, true to our decidedly different natures.

It was the summer vacation that never ended. I wandered the property with a book or sat on the dock paddling my feet in the water. I contacted friends more, walked in woods and meadow. I spent more time at the computer, often looking up to see the neighbour's cows pass by my window single file, as I got back to writing.

For Carl, glad as he had been to retire, the quiet was not renewing. His legs might be shaky and his balance a bit off, but he had always been a man who came home after work and chopped wood or mowed lawns. He looked around for something to do. Carl had been a creative and caring teacher. He had inspired a lot of young minds. But teaching had not been his first choice of jobs.

"What do you really want to do?" I asked.

"I'm tired of being a white collar worker. I want to be 'plaid'."

He put on old flannel shirts and a ball cap and spent a summer working with a landscaper. His back ached, but his mind rejoiced at being a *dirt-guy*. My image of him planting little flowers and bushes vanished with his descriptions of wheelbarrows full of cement and truckloads of mulch. But for that summer Carl enjoyed the camaraderie of working with other men. They kept a radio on and laughed at the silliness of CBC radio's *Dead Dog Café*. Their days often extended until eight at night, but Carl was happier than I'd ever seen him. 'Plaid' was good.

A 'V' and an 'X'

I liked to stand at the kitchen sink and look at the lake below through a deep V in the trees. Each season begged for a photographer to capture it. Trees in winter white or blazing orange, mist rising from the lake. "You must never take this view for granted," I reminded myself.

We welcomed the beautiful new surroundings as we adjusted to living in the forest (good) and longer drives to work (not as good). Moving forces change. But while we had volunteered for our particular changes, up on the Bruce Peninsula farm where Carl was raised, his parents were finding themselves pulled towards less welcome changes as they could no longer manage the farm where they had spent most of their lives.

Had they left it too long? Carl's Dad had struggled with health issues for many years by now and he and Grandma Katie were past eighty. Increasingly they spent their days in the bright yellow kitchen where in winter, thick woolen socks hung to dry above the wood stove and in summer the heavy windows balanced on thin sticks, propping them open for a breeze to flow through. Katie sang to herself as she put dishes in the cupboards. At five foot eight she could reach fairly well but those cupboards stretched to the ceilings. And the rickety basement stairs were hardly safe for someone Katie's age. It was time for them to move into town, closer to a hospital and grocery shopping, and an easier way of living.

As Carl's sister Helen and I cleaned out accumulations of forty years from the old brick farm house, Carl sorted junk from treasures in outbuildings and went through unsettling changes of his own. Through that summer he felt more and more unwell, falling asleep at odd times and in odd places. While we visited with neighbours following a potluck dinner, it was not unusual to find Carl sprawled across the carpet asleep. Why did we not see this as a warning sign?

We did not connect Carl's falling asleep to the sore which developed on his bottom. It was late September before anyone realized that Carl had an E-coli infection. With this happening a couple of years prior to the Walkerton Tragedy, people were less conscious of e-coli infections, and until Carl became sick, we did not understand how dangerous this illness could be. The doctor called with blood test results one Thursday just before choir practice. Carl needed to go directly to hospital and stay overnight in preparation for surgery the following morning. "You go to choir practice," Carl insisted, "I'm fine."

I tried to focus on teaching the choir but could not keep my mind on either music or people. Finally I confessed to the group why I was so distracted. Several of the singers gasped, "What on earth are you doing here? Get in to that hospital. Your place is with your husband." Duty is a strong call for me. I had needed permission to be where I wanted to be. Gratefully I drove to town.

Despite his earlier insistence, Carl's face relaxed in obvious relief when I entered the hospital room. We needed to be together.

Surgery went fine, with the removal of a large section of Carl's backside. Family and friends had long joked that Carl's pants were likely to fall down because "he had no bum." Truly there wasn't much of a backside to spare, and here they were, taking some away.

Carl was hospitalized for a week and a half. With his good friend Dave also recuperating from surgery in the same hospital, nurses learned quickly that when either patient went missing they need only look down the hall in the other's room. Once Carl was discharged, home care nurses, the first of many he would come to know, navigated the bush road for several weeks, calling cheerful greetings as they flung the door open. Not a nurse by nature, I was considerably relieved at their presence and skill, as again and again they packed the wound with yards of sterile gauze, a sort of "placeholder" for missing tissue. The thought of a huge hole in my husband's body was alien at best, frightening at worst.

But the body can hold such healing power. Weeks passed, and the nurses began expressing satisfaction that the amount of packing was decreasing. In the end, Carl was left with a large "X marks the spot" on his bottom.

Present Friend, Absent Husband

Do other couples carry on a lifelong discussion the way Carl and I seemed to? We talked on the lawn swing, on the deck, on the couch, in the car. Our chosen topic was friendship. Through years of conversations we decided that friendship exists only where there is vulnerability and trust. I agree with author Madeleine L'Engle's words on the subject: "When we were children, we used to think that when we were grown-up we would no longer be vulnerable. But to grow up is to accept vulnerability ... to be alive is to be vulnerable."

Carl and I had always been best friends, able to be honest with one another. But there are great risks in throwing yourself open to another person. You walk a tightrope, seeking balance between sensitivity and defenselessness. When I was fourteen, my next door neighbour wrote about vulnerability and secrets in my autograph book:

> *Never to your friends impart the hidden secrets of your heart; For if your friends become your foes, the whole world your secret knows.*

With the telling and not telling of secrets, the heart has its own wisdom, but it does need some input from the brain. I am cautious about how much I share and with whom. In addition to having Carl as my best friend, I am blessed with several close women friends. And we take trust and vulnerability for granted in the safe space of each other's company. For example, not much escapes my friend Ruth. If I didn't tell her my sorrows she would see them anyway. She is the kind of friend who just listens and asks the questions you need in order to think your way out of your sadness. I don't know where she learned how to be a friend. She just seems to know.

Years ago I was marking papers at my desk after school when I heard a grade two teacher in the hallway clearly exasperated with her small pupil: 'to *have* a friend, you must *be* a friend'. That brings the whole question to its simplest terms.

> *A friend is someone who knows the song in your heart, and can sing it back to you when you have forgotten the words.*
>
> Unknown

I had previously known the *song in Carl's heart* but I wasn't sure of it anymore. He was changing in many ways, both physically and emotionally. And I felt he was absent from our marriage. I missed him. I missed talking over our problems and making decisions together. Often I would walk the bush road out to the highway about the time I expected him home in the evening. I left the house with a spring in my step eager for the chance to share the happenings of our day on the drive back to the house. But most often I walked back alone. Slower. Sadder. I realized that I needn't stay in the dark place I was currently in. But I wanted Carl beside me to help me find my way out.

Despite being an avid reader, I never read love stories until I immersed myself in *The Bridges of Madison County*, identifying so strongly with this woman who was saying goodbye to the love of her life. As I read, I wondered if I was leaving Carl. I wondered if his emotional absence meant that he was leaving me. I was bewildered at the state of our marriage and in the dark as to how to restore it.

The Bridges of Madison County was a quick read but it stayed in my head and would not let me go. Whatever did my soul have in common with Francesca Johnson? We were both in mid-life, wives and mothers. There the commonality ended. Francesca had married a good man but there was no spark in the marriage. When Robert Kincaid came into her life she gave herself wholeheartedly to him, and then sacrificed her chance at happiness choosing ... what? The steady, comforting ritual of her familiar life? Her children? A husband who could not see who she really was?

I could feel how it was to be Francesca, on that sweltering summer day, crickets singing, the air hazy with heat. But I would never be found lounging on my verandah with iced tea in hand, awaiting the arrival of an extraordinary stranger to waken me from a lifelong dream state. I had the only man I had ever wanted. Except that we were not seeing one another much.

When Francesca turned her back on Robert Kincaid, when she watched through the rain streaked truck window as he disappeared from her life, it was still — for her — a choice. I thought a lot about the choices I was making, staying in a relationship with a man I saw for only a few waking hours a week. I thought about the love Francesca and Robert Kincaid had, and even if it was only for a few days, and even if they were fictional characters, I envied them.

I knew where there was a covered bridge like the one in the book. I had plenty of time to myself, with Carl gone dawn to dusk. So on one of those rare warm autumn days when winter seems far in the future, I got out my map of Southwestern Ontario and went looking for the bridge. I found it, a length of weathered red boards, and next to it a parking lot where a handful of young men from a wedding party were quietly changing into tuxedos from the trunk of their car. They were on their way to a ceremony celebrating the beginning of a life together. *Was I at this bridge to observe some ceremony of my own?*

Once the young people left, I had the bridge to myself. I looked at it from every angle. I imagined Francesca at one end of the bridge, and Robert Kincaid photographing her from the other end. I wanted Carl here to see it with me, to stroll around it under the Indian summer sky, and hear the cicadas singing for that single day. I hated that he was two hours away. Working. Not even knowing where his wife was. I began feeling pathetic and melancholy. Bridges lead somewhere. I longed for a bridge back, or even better, forward, to my marriage.

Take This Job, or...

Years earlier we had invested all our money and much of our energy into buying and putting an addition on a property in the wrong location at the wrong time. Forced by a real estate crash into becoming landlords we watched helplessly as year after year went by with the house unsold. We paid the taxes. We paid the insurance. We repaired the latest tenant-damage. One tenant ran the well dry and neighbours shook their heads: "That hasn't happened in a hundred years."

At the grocery store we put on a brave face, nickel and diming it. Our family went without new clothes for years and made homemade gifts every Christmas. There were no Value Village Stores in those days. A financial situation like this one meant that a big meal out was a trip to MacDonald's with a two-for-one certificate. Years passed and our little girl never got a new dress.

Now that little girl was leaving for university. The best we could do was to go to the bank for loans and give each of our children a start, their first year's schooling paid for. After that they would be on their own. As is the way of these things, our car had to be replaced at a time we could least afford it.

Carl, especially, seemed to be standing on a shaky foundation, and not just financially. "Sometimes my legs feel like jelly," he told me. I did not understand what he was trying to get across. And neither of us recognized the importance of his words. It would be another fifteen years before anyone, doctors included, figured out what was going on with Carl's legs. For now, we were more worried about making our car payments.

Contrary to the whisperings of my heart, but out of financial concern, I considered a position with a large city church. I sat on the organ bench while the interviewing committee surrounded me.

Unconsciously I was probably doing my best not to get the position. "I'm worried about the liturgy," I admitted. "Your church is ten times more formal than any church I have ever worked for."

"For the first weeks," said one of the men, "I could sit here with you to let you get used to where in the service the responses are played." I was still nervous. "Do you understand I am a generalist? I can do most things reasonably well, but I'm not trained to the degree you might have been used to in the past. And I wonder about taking on too much with my husband having health concerns." I hoped I was not exaggerating, but reminded myself that even with the e-coli infection healing, Carl's legs seemed weak and shaky. I might need time to take on a larger share of work at home in future.

The rector heard the worry beneath my words. "What part of the job do you like doing best?" he asked. I grasped at the straw being offered: "I'm strongest at choir work," I suggested, "and I'd rather play piano than organ." My mind scolded: how was this going to work? Piano was useful for many things but they used a pipe organ for services. I had played a pipe organ for fifteen years at a previous job, and knew that reluctant or not, I could manage. The men tossed ideas back and forth. If I did not do much work with the organ it would mean they needed two musicians instead of one. To my surprise someone said "We think that could be arranged. You go home and think about it."

For three days the decision to leave the small village church fifteen minutes from home weighed heavy on my mind. I shuffled through fallen leaves along the bush road imagining two futures. In the large church we would meet new people and even a job-sharing situation would mean a sizable salary increase. But the struggling congregation in Shallow Lake needed me so much more. The church board gave me complete freedom to do the job as I saw fit and the work was easy there, whereas if I took the city job, there was the intimidating unfamiliar liturgy to be learned.

By Sunday paying the bills had won out. I would accept the new job. At coffee hour I sat down with the chair of the board in a corner of the church basement. "We will do anything to keep you here," he said, and in an instant the decision was un-made once more. "What if we add modern hymn books to our resources and increase your salary to a level where you have some reasonable choice?"

I called the rector of the city church, that afternoon, feeling pulled in opposite directions. I heard the kindness in his voice. "With your husband's health concerns, do you perhaps have enough on your plate already?" he asked. My shoulders lowered two inches from their tensed up position as I accepted the verbal life preserver. I would remain a big frog in a little puddle.

Soul Neglected (Carl Sleeps)

The next April, our real estate experiment-gone-wrong finally sold and we felt the weight of an eleven-year burden lifted from our shoulders. I could give up standing in the aisle of the grocery store looking for the cheapest can of peas. We could afford to stop for supper on the way home when we went to visit Catherine in Toronto. I felt more free than I had in a long time.

Carl had put the days of visiting nurses behind him and returned to reasonably good health over the winter. He should have been a happy man, I thought, but instead his mood became increasingly dark.

I read uplifting books where the authors talked about trust and love. Those were the forces I needed in my life if I was to face the gathering fear I felt, watching Carl slip into obvious depression. I felt bewildered and confused. *Why was my husband so gloomy?* Eleven years of worry removed, and yet Carl reacts with a bleak melancholy. It made no sense to me.

For two months I had struggled with a queasy stomach and a fist-like sensation just above the navel. One evening I made my way through the narrow rock cut we called Weightwatchers' Gap and wandered down to the dock clutching a library book about angels. Sitting on a weather worn chair I divided my attention between lake and book. No water skiers, no boats, just the still surface of the water.

As I turned the pages, I came upon a mantra. Nobody around to hear me. I gave a mental shrug, and sang out the unfamiliar syllables several times. "Ee nu rah," I intoned. "Ee nu rah, Ee nu rah, zay." This last syllable drawn out. Then I changed pitch to a half tone higher. My voice sounded strangely hollow and distant to my ears.

I scanned the horizon across the water. Was the sky darker? How long had I been sitting there? Puzzled, I folded up the creaky lawn-chair, tucked the book beneath one arm and started the climb back up to the house.

When I woke up the next morning, the *fist* in my stomach was gone. It seemed to me that the fist represented Carl's pain and that all spring I had been somehow taking it in to my own body. Sitting on the dock the night before I had unconsciously released the ache, which I decided did not belong to me and had no business settling in my stomach. It was gone and it felt right that it was gone.

As good as it felt to be free of the discomfort, I still worried about Carl. Should I draw back? Should I push him to explore emotional issues he had shoved under the carpet? If I made him talk it out was this an unhealthy entangling of our emotional lives? An old wooden lawn swing stood by the edge of the cliff. Here we spent many summer evenings, talking and listening and talking some more, and when the cool of the fall intervened, we moved our discussions indoors.

Between discussions I read Thomas Moore's Care of the Soul. 'When soul is neglected it doesn't just go away. It appears symptomatically in obsessions, addictions, violence, and loss of meaning.' Loss of meaning! Wasn't this what Carl was experiencing? It made sense to me to think that there were as Moore suggested, 'necessary changes requested by depression and anxiety.' Depression in Carl's case. Anxiety in mine. Each of us triggering the other's unhelpful reaction, cycling round and round. *But what were the necessary changes?*

Carl moved into an angry place where I could not and would not follow. Although at the time, it seemed to me that he was running away from me, it was really his own shadow he sought to elude. He only knew he felt hollow inside. But the man I knew had been replaced by a different man, one whose anger held me at bay. A sudden flaming anger I might have fought, but this slow seething bitterness just made me want to run.

Each night after a quick supper he escaped into sleep, getting up at 4:30 the next morning to drive into town and sit in coffee shops with strangers. I think some part of him was reaching out to be with others, but *sitting near* is not *being with*. I wondered if entering his world would bring us closer so one morning I went with him. Sitting at the bare table with hot drinks in our hands I looked around the building where we knew no one. He pointed out people he had seen before but not ever spoken with. I looked for meaning and found none. It seemed so much lonelier than being alone.

I felt lost. Inaction becoming a crippling force in my life. I could not think what to do. I knew *what ifs* were not enough, but could not see the *what nexts*. I reminded myself of Mark Twain's wry comment: 'My life has been filled with terrible misfortunes, most of which never happened.' But this misfortune was happening. As the most vibrant relationship of my life crumbled around me, I watched helplessly.

Through the winter it seemed as if Carl had gone into hibernation. His sleeping form stretched out on the couch in front of a television. He didn't care what program was on. To him the background noise served as a lullaby. Every evening I watched him escape into sleep, then retreated to the other end of the house. If I had to feel this isolation, I would make a statement about the separation by going somewhere else. It was the reaction of an abandoned child. While Carl dozed on the couch by the woodstove, I sat alone listening to music in the cold sitting room, wrapped in blankets, a book for company. *How many more months would I be able to continue in a marriage with the stranger Carl had become?*

The loss of my best friend was changing my way of being in the world. Where once Carl and I had enjoyed craft shows together, I now went to them alone. Increasingly I sought out family and friends. I sorted through my concerns while walking in the woods and meadow. My journals took on a more honest tone. Previously I would not have recorded feelings I believed unworthy. For example, times I felt frustrated I had not written that down because I thought the negative feelings did not deserve to be put down on paper. Now I described myself in my journal as a 'worrier filled with indecision and crippled by inertia.'

I knew I could not stay in this dark emotional space. I had a solid base of feeling loved to fall back on. My parents had loved me. My husband had loved me (and still did, somewhere beneath the murky shadows of his melancholy.) There were new understandings I needed to reach: I must learn to ask for what I wanted and needed. Certainly nothing in my marriage, prior to Carl's depression, led me to neglecting my own needs. But if I expected Carl to explore his dark places, then I had better be willing to look at my own. "What is a dark night of the soul?" I asked a minister friend one day. Instantly his demeanour switched from light conversation to quiet intensity. "It is the worst thing you go through, all the worst things," he said softly. "And we may have more than one of them in the course of our lifetime."

With spring, Carl met a new friend Rick and the two men began doing carpentry projects together. Carl had worked so hard to build 'the house that wouldn't sell' and with that eleven year journey behind us I half expected him to wash his hands of building things altogether. But building and selling garden arbors provided a kick-start to Carl's stalled self-esteem. Working with a partner was ideal at a time when Carl was not as physically able as he used to be. It worked well for Rick too as Carl had always been a people person and had a wide circle of acquaintances who just might need a hand with yard-work or carpentry projects.

Without any real effort the jobs came in and soon the two men were doing yard-work and small renovations for a variety of people over a widening geographic area. Carl was happier. But he was also gone from home twelve to thirteen hours a day. His current tiredness no longer came from depression, but from doing demanding physical work. Still he slept. Little had changed for me.

One summer evening as the last golden rays of sun slid beneath the trees I closed the door and crossed the yard. The forest surrounding the house would be dark any minute, but another hour of day remained in the fields above. I wandered up the cow path in my nightgown and a long plaid shirt, moving aimlessly through the long grass. Dusk fell and suddenly I was surrounded by fireflies. I longed to have my husband with me to share my delight. But back on his couch Carl slept on, unaware. I made my way back through meadow and forest and crawled into bed. Around two-thirty in the morning I was awakened by a flash of light in the bedroom. A firefly had hitched a ride on my long nightgown.

Is It All Right?

It seemed to me that Carl wore his negative feelings like a cloak, wrapping fear and sadness around his being and clutching them to him. My sadness took a different form. It went into words, forming poems I had not known were there. "I am the reluctant poet," I told a friend. "If I wrapped a cloak of sadness around me the words would thump and bump against it until they found a way out."

Winter took hold, sending my husband home earlier in the day. At last there was time to concentrate on one another. Lying on the bed, candles lit, electric stove warming the room, we talked a lot about our day-to-day life, but didn't say much that was new. My song was, "Stay with me, stay with me." Carl's answer was, "I gotta be free." On some level, though, we were hearing one another. One night Carl turned to me and said: "There's no you and no me. There's just us." My mind could not reconcile this surprising announcement with the long absences of the previous summer or the hours spent hiding in sleep the previous winter. Beneath the words, his feelings were sincere, but it still seemed to me that "Just us" was in danger of crumbling.

Many barn roofs collapsed under the weight of wet snow before one of the longest winters in memory came to an end. Gradually I observed the days grow longer and waited for snow, and then mud, to give way to green. With spring's arrival Carl resumed his marathon work hours, and again we saw less and less of one another. The sad discussions of the previous six months had yielded little permanent change in the down-spiraling pattern of our marriage. "What happened to 'Just Us'?" I wondered. My husband was missing in action again in the daytime, and asleep on the couch in the evenings. It felt demeaning, begging him to spend time with me, but I did it anyway.

My view of marriage was undoubtedly carved out of childhood experience. I had seen my parents separated by my father's death when my mother was only thirty-eight. Theirs was a loving relationship. When Dad went for a walk he usually brought back a treat for Mom. He teased her about cutting the brick of ice cream crooked and said she needed round loaves of bread so she could have as many crusts as she wanted. Often I heard them laughing together after lights out.

Before this, laughter had been part of our marriage too. In earlier years we went to summer theater whenever we could. Always the comedies. We sat in the darkened theater holding hands and in some ways I preferred watching Carl, head thrown back, laughing at the antics on stage, to watching the play.

Carl had always liked to make me laugh. When the kids were small he would lift them off the floor by placing a forearm on each shoulder and a hand on each ear. But first he would inquire solemnly: "Have you been doing your ear-ups?" with a sly glance sideways to see if I was enjoying the production.

I missed the laughter. The teasing, outrageous Carl I had always known had been replaced by a man who wanted very little more in life than to be out somewhere with other men working. In his need to be part of that other world he had removed himself from my world. I was not willing to throw our history away by suggesting a separation. Still the separation was there ... an emotional separation. The year before, when we had been distanced by his depression, we hadn't quite recognized it for what it was or noticed the damage it was inflicting. Time spent together in the winter months had not been enough to rebuild my connection to him.

As spring moved into summer I felt increasingly isolated. I began running away from home. Not for long times, but frequently, I tucked my journal and a pen into my purse, jumped into the car, and took off down the road. There was a relief in the running. It felt like doing something after months of inertia. So I ran. I ran to the field, to the highway, to our daughter's place. I sat on hills and in parks and looked out at the water. After a while, in whichever refuge I sought, Carl, with a newfound strength, began to come looking for me.

The forest around the house had grown dark but up in the meadow the sun still shone. I didn't want to wait in the house for Carl to come home. I needed someplace else to be, so I sat on a fallen log in the meadow, journal in hand. For the first time in my life I examined what I needed most: a balance of time for self, family, and friends. A connection with like-minded friends who would love books as I did, and value discussing ideas. I thought about the needs of family members too, staying especially conscious of Carl's health. 'I may lose what I have,' I wrote. I feared this possibility but I knew that whatever changes were happening to Carl health-wise were out of my control, and very likely out of his.

The sun shone on my face, and as I wrote the *aha!* moments came more often. "I need to re-state *Is it all right if I want this?* and instead say, *This is what I want and it's all right.*"

Whenever Carl was away working with Rick, there was no way to predict when he would get home. Supper for me had been two hours ago. His meal sat on top of the stove drying and shrivelled up. Once he had eaten he would make his way up to the meadow to sit with me for a little, telling me about his day, asking about mine.

Slowly he was becoming a different and happier person, finally fighting for his survival as the person he had once been or the new person he wanted to be. "I have to put myself first right now," he told me. He wanted more than anything in the world to feel competent and capable. Being out in the world building things, was how he was achieving this feeling. His time went to shovels and mowers, moss and trees and lawns.

He could see how his absence was affecting me, but for now he saw no choice. In me, old feelings of unworthiness surfaced. If I was not a priority in my husband's mind, then did I really matter to anyone? Carl had *himself* back, but that did not mean I had my *husband* back.

Divider

Dragged into view the bricks of sadness, hurt, and loss.
Mixed with our tears, the mortar of misunderstanding.
Shaped (or mis-shaped?) the constraining wall between us:
barrier, impediment, obstacle to gentle touch or deep connection.
Wobbling thinly on unsteady ground,
unsightly, unbecoming, uninviting ... and unwanted.
While both of us cry behind it:
"Can you still see me? Can you still see me?"

The Remedy for Suffering

"There is only one thing I want for our thirtieth anniversary," I told Carl, "an afternoon with you, and an evening with some old friends." With a picnic basket of sandwiches and cookies and two pretty china mugs Katie had given us as a gift for the special day, I made my way down the winding path to the water's edge. Carl had promised to be home by noon. We would have a whole afternoon together.

The big wooden lawn swing where we once talked our way through Carl's depression still stood on the cliff above, but down at the dock we had a second swing, tiny and made from metal. I still remember Carl shaking his head when I unloaded it from the car. "It's second hand and it was only $10.00," I exclaimed, "I can use it down by the lake." And use it I did, despite the fact that no cushions known to mankind would fit it. I watched at yard sales for cheap chair cushions and set them side by side along the metal frame, jigsaw fashion. There was not enough room for three cushions. Two and a half would have been perfect. The answer seemed to be two with a six inch gap between them. We could each sit at one end, a space between us. Seemed fitting.

That day by the lake we ate our picnic lunch and Carl gave me a gold necklace with the number thirty on it. I still wear it sometimes to remind myself how close we came to losing one another in that thirtieth year. Even as he fastened the necklace I wondered if the thirty would be a sad reminder some day, but for now I wanted just to enjoy our time together. My gift for him was a cell phone, a device for better communication. It was a gift he wanted, but the irony did not escape me. We climbed back up the trail to the house and changed our clothes. The two destinations we had in mind for the afternoon, were the old McNeill Estate on the escarpment above

Colpoy's Bay, and further north, Bruce Beckons, an antique shop in a log cabin. We liked antiques. Our house was furnished with enough of them, but mostly because of our fondness for wooden furniture rather than for their antique value.

Bruce Beckons displayed things historical, and often made visitors welcome with a cup of hot apple cider. No apple cider this warm August day though. Just a stroll around the grounds. In addition to antiques the owners were clearly fond of animals. Rabbits hopped around the lawn. Baby goats cried in high-pitched voices and small funny fowl stepped lightly across the hard ground on fuzzy slippered feet. The weather could not have been more beautiful. I took photos, wanting memories of this special day together.

We had invited members of our wedding party for dinner at the lodge where we had celebrated our marriage in nineteen-seventy-one. We were delighted to find that the tree from our wedding photos was still there and the six of us took turns posing and snapping pictures. Then we walked along the rocky Huron shoreline chatting and enjoying the sunset. It felt like being married again after a summer of distance. It was these rare flashes of the way we used to be which sustained me in my lost condition that summer.

The events of September eleven overshadowed for a while, our personal concerns. A friend and I returned from a happily oblivious morning at the Keady market, to the horrendous story unfolding on television. Michael met us at the door: "America is under attack!" he exclaimed. I waited for the next line, thinking it was a joke. We sat in the family room with bowls of soup, watching the planes hit the buildings again and again in never ending replays, and we tried to comprehend how our world had changed.

How did our neighbour nation and our own absorb the shocking scenes of bodies tumbling from buildings, the sorrow of people holding up pictures of their surely lost loved ones? For comfort I turned to the written word. I needed to hear what wiser minds than mine were thinking. I prayed for the wisdom to help others feel safe, knowing that when any one is threatened, nobody is really safe.

Pulling a thin volume from my bedroom bookcase I turned to Gary Zukav's writings for guidance, and then sat down at the computer to look for his website: 'The remedy for an absence is a presence. Where there is evil, do what you can, using the energy of Love,' he wrote, and 'Look with compassion on those who have suffered and those who have committed acts of cruelty alike, then you will see that all are suffering. The remedy for suffering is not to inflict more suffering.' Days went by with people feeling out of sorts. On the radio they talked about the *new normal*. We held onto small things … anything positive to counterbalance the negative week our world had been through.

I was delighted to see eleven egrets in the Shallow Lake swamp, and I watched for the slender white forms every time I passed. They were a distraction, but not for long. The sun still shone. The sky remained blue. But my mind, and perhaps everyone else's too, returned again and again to planes hitting buildings. The internet was my lifeline, showing me what the wise people of our world were thinking and feeling about the September eleven attacks. A quote from Matthew B. offered me much comfort: 'Out of chaos comes new creation.' The sharing of such thoughts seemed to offer the only sense possible to make out of the tragedy.

I knew little about Matthew B. Like me he was a writer and musician. I had stumbled upon his website a few weeks earlier. New to the internet and unsure of what was and was not appropriate, I only knew I needed to reach out to somebody. Here was a clear thinking and compassionate person, and as odd as it felt to write to someone I did not know at all, I had sent a note a week or two earlier telling him about the changes in Carl, and my sorrow and confusion.

As lost as I might feel, I had in reaching out into the universe for help, chosen the right person. He wrote back right away, a validating letter cautioning that I seemed to be too 'entangled' with my husband's feelings. Not only was this co-dependence harmful to me, but it was not what Carl needed. "Unfortunately, such behaviour also subtly encourages the other person to NOT deal with their own issues, and supports them in suppressing their own feelings," wrote the kind stranger. "Have you considered setting some spiritual goals?" The question would change my life. In my journal soon after, I noted that 'I don't so much choose the goals as have them chosen for me. And I know that I had spiritual goals before. I just wasn't aware of them.'

Through this time in September with the world turned upside down I used journaling to explore my thoughts and feelings. Sometimes I leafed through an old journal looking for words which might seem to jump out and strike me as meaningful. Other times I followed a pattern of reviewing what I had written exactly a year ago. What goals might help me become more compassionate, more aware?

I wondered about releasing attachment to other people's opinions. Often I had told Carl I didn't really care what people thought about me or my choices. Right. How honest was that? I didn't think I could handle *detachment* as a goal. Maybe I would start with *observing behaviour without judging it*. I thought I might be able to keep from judging others, maybe even terrorists. Sadly, I didn't think I could keep from judging myself.

The chill of autumn was settling in. By late afternoon the forest outside cast its shadow into the house and in the dim family room I curled up each day in the large padded rocker, across from the old wood stove. On the blanket box in front of me I had arranged and lit candles. There were tea lights in glass jars, and tapers in white metal holders. Tinfoil cuffs hugged their bases so they would not fall over. One fat red candle was left over from the previous Christmas.

The scene was far from a decorator's idea of arranging candles. Nothing matched. It didn't have to. But always I included a heavy hollowed out cube which had been a gift from friends as a reminder that they were thinking of us. A wavering light shone through the brilliant royal blue glass. The world post 9-11 was dark. But in my own little world, the stove glowed warm and my mismatched collection of candles shone bravely. I needed all the light I could get.

"While You're Making Other Plans"

Through the previous summer Carl's legs had become increasingly shaky and he began to lose his balance more often, occasionally stumbling. Doing rough outdoor work often involved cutting across uneven ground so that Carl's legs were usually scarred from spills when he couldn't regain his balance. "My legs feel like jelly," he so often told me. Not being an athlete at any time in my life I couldn't identify but I knew we had seen these symptoms eight years earlier. "Could I have MS?" Carl had wondered then, and though no cause had been found last time, we stepped cautiously onto the slow road of getting a diagnosis, knowing instinctively that we were in for a rough ride. An appointment with a neurologist was made amidst a heightening of our personal anxieties. "Let go of things you can't control," I reminded myself. We needed to plan for what we could control.

A day or two before Thanksgiving I opened the china cabinet drawer and pulled out the yellow felt turkey head our friend Bonnie had made for us. I tipped a fresh pineapple over on its side and fastened the head to one end with toothpicks to form a body and tail. There had been years when Carl stuck small garden mums in with the tail, and our Thanksgiving turkey became a Thanksgiving peacock.

Two family dinners early that weekend filled our table with leftovers and friends for the next few days. We all loved hot turkey sandwiches, but the kids and I most looked forward every year to our all time favourite leftover dish, Carl's turkey croquettes. Carl didn't cook much anymore and I missed standing side by side stirring whatever was on the stove top.

I wondered what changes lay around the corner and I tried to convince myself there would be possibilities in whatever lay ahead. I had been longing for time with my husband and part of me worried: *am I going to be given time with Carl in a way neither of us wants? Is a time coming when he will be home with me more because he is no longer able to be out working?* I was pretty sure Carl was wondering the same thing.

When test results from the neurologist were unbearably slow in reaching us I decided to take a stand.

"This is not appropriate," I told our young doctor. To my surprise he agreed with me.

"You're right. It's not appropriate. You will hear from me soon."

Carl was not home when I took the call saying his CT scan suggested a brain tumour or aneurysm. While the doctor tried to arrange an appointment with a Toronto specialist, I scribbled down notes concerning approaching appointments and commitments. I would update friends that evening and pack in the morning for a trip to a specialist, I decided. But *life is what happens while you're making other plans*. The doctor called back. We were to rush to Toronto immediately.

Frantic phone calls to find Carl yielded no response, but friends I spoke with encouraged me to prepare for the trip right away. Carl's lifelong friend Dave Greig offered to drive us down, and neighbour-friend Cathy arrived to help me pack. Carl pulled in to the driveway, expecting the normal hum of supper preparations. Instead I met him on the steps, portable phone still in hand, urging him to hurry as they were waiting for us in Toronto. In the back of my mind was the feeling that he could be in imminent danger. *Do aneurysms explode?*

I had promised Dave that I was a good navigator, but the dark night limited my map reading skills considerably. Once we reached the city we relied on a mixture of what parts of the map I was able to make out in the darkness and what any of the three of us could recall about Toronto streets.

Carl was placed in a curtained area with Dave and I dragging along a thirty pound hockey bag of belongings Cathy had helped me throw together. She had foreseen that this would not be a single night stay, but our choices had been confused at best. *Weird underwear* was how Carl later described the assortment of old briefs which were the only ones we could find for him. By one in the morning, with Carl finally admitted, we sent Dave off to find a bed and I faced what was left of the night in a chair.

Eventually a nurse told me I could lie down in a small common room at the other end of the floor. I arranged my lumpy purse under my head, stuck my feet through the wooden armrest at the end of the five foot plastic couch, and drew my jacket over me. The discovery of gloves in the jacket pocket was a happy one as they went inside the purse to cushion pill bottles, wallet, and other contents of the bag. I would guess these to include a hairbrush, pen and notebook, lipstick, but they felt more like lumps of coal and small branches from the forest.

With the gloves placed strategically over the sharper items, I lay my head on the purse and closed my eyes. It was about a quarter to three in the morning. Around four, a nurse woke me to offer a real pillow and a sheet. The words 'ministering angel' came into my head.

>Oct.17 journal entry:
>
>My father's birthday today ... and we are at Toronto Western Hospital after a wearisome night. My eyes are burning from lack of sleep. Carl waits for an MRI. In the next bed an old gent calls out "I see the light!" and then bursts into one line of *You Light up My Life*. Single lines are all he does but they are quite tuneful. We have already heard *You are my Sunshine* and *Shine on Harvest Moon*.
>
>When breakfast arrives, he informs the woman who delivers it, that she is an "angel of mercy". From my experience the night before I identify with this thought readily enough. "Who's that knocking at my door?" sings out the old gentleman. Carl remembers that the car is to be painted Monday. Might need to get that appointment cancelled or make other arrangements. "I'm not in the mood!" calls the old man. Right!
>
>A large gowned figure enters the room. I am not sure if she is staff or a patient and neither is the old man, who asks her about this. It is even harder for him to figure

out as he is blind. "I'm the nurse," she tells him. "The curse?" he inquires while we stifle giggles. Then he gives us a chorus of *You Always Hurt the One You Love*. When she asks him what he'd like to do after breakfast he is quite clear: "Hold hands with you all day. I'm a romantic at heart," and then he sings out *I Wonder Who's Kissing Her Now!*

Suddenly, the room is a flurry of activity with two nurses and a doctor. "Were you a sergeant in the women's army?" asks the old man of one nurse. "You sure are good at giving orders!" A while passes and there are (obviously fake) snorting sounds from behind the curtain divider, and then the exclamation: "I'm snoring!"

Each female who enters the room is romanced. Jim (we have learned his name) does not play favourites. "Wine, women and song," he tells one, is his motto. He asks for their phone numbers and advises them that they'd better "run for their life!" Often he calls for Lorraine, a nurse we have not met, and a departing nurse is serenaded with *Let Me Call You Sweetheart*, followed with a medley of Christmas songs punctuated by loud drilling from the roof above us.

As Jim's medications are brought in, he launches into *I Hear Music When I Think of You*. Frankly, I'd guess that Jim hears music when he thinks of anything!

By noon, Carl's sister Helen and husband Jack arrived to wait with us for Carl's MRI to be done. Hospital staff warned that it could happen in the middle of the night since this valuable equipment is kept in constant use.

I am somewhat *directionally challenged*. I thought this was my secret until I noted that Jack and Helen kept up a description of our surroundings anytime we left the hospital: "Let's go towards the CN Tower," and "We'll just walk along in front of that school." On the first occasion where I needed to walk alone, I encountered Jack halfway, by accident, he said. I can just imagine the conversation in that hospital room that afternoon: "You don't think she might get lost do you?" "Maybe somebody should go down and look for her."

A trip for the MRI in the wee hours of the morning was aborted when there was concern over whether Carl had ever had metal fragments in his eyes. This, we learned, could be disastrous, and so there was a delay to allow for an x-ray just to be sure. Carl, after all, could be described as rather accident prone, and over the years had a generous share of unusual mishaps. Hatchets missed their intended targets and slit fingers. Buckets of plaster positioned themselves ready to be stepped in below ladders. Klinkers jumped out of woodstoves and burned unmentionable parts of his body. A nursing student friend compiled a whole year of case studies based on Carl alone. When it came to the possibility of metal fragments in the eye, it was safer to check.

While Carl went for the MRI the next morning, Helen and I strolled the short distance to Kensington Market. We bought fresh vegetables for that night's supper, and looked forward to the reassuring activity of cooking for ourselves, using the little microwave oven at the hotel.

Carl had been warned about the loud sounds he would be subjected to during the test, but he found the level of noise disconcerting. Attention deficit disorder runs in the family, and while Carl has learned to cope with that difference, he is more sensitive in sight and hearing than most of us are. He tried to predict when the next clamour would occur, and count the seconds between, reminding himself that the whole procedure would be over in about twenty minutes. He did not want to use the kill switch they had given him, a rescue strategy which would abort the test in case the patient became too panicky.

It was late evening before the specialist was able to get to us. We heard only one word of his first sentence: dramatic.

> Oct. 19 journal entry:
>
> Shocking results from Carl's MRI. His brain stem is being pushed back by a blood vessel which is twisted into an abnormal shape. This is so rare that Dr. Thapar has only heard of one case before. We're all feeling somewhat stunned.

Riding the Coaster

We arrived home from Toronto to find Rick nailing up a pine ceiling in our sunroom, and Carl immediately picked up a hammer, comforted by the familiar work. The phone rang and Cathy informed me that there was a turkey in her oven, which we were welcome to share up there. "But if," she continued, "you are just thankful to be home in your own little house, I will bring plates of supper down to you."

Cathy and I often called one another late in the afternoon and pooled resources for potluck suppers. If it was a spur of the moment thing we would have just our two families. Other times we would plan further ahead and invite a larger group. Sitting around a table sharing food and conversation provided spiritual as well as physical sustenance.

In those first days back at home, Cathy was one of three friends who dropped down often. Neighbour Ruth and I took walks down the bush road in the cold November afternoons and then she would come back to the house to visit with Carl. Dave kept in touch with Carl by phone and stopped in for visits. These were friends who shared to some degree our family's emotional roller coaster. But they and I rode the roller coaster voluntarily where Carl had no choice.

More than ever now Carl needed friends to be with, to talk to, to widen a world now narrowed by health concerns, but seeing concern in people's faces was too painful. Phone calls were easier for the first week or two. "Good afternoon. Bass Lake Brainstem Research Center," Carl would say into the receiver while I shuddered inwardly at the dark humour. We had different ways of handling what was happening. There was no manual to teach us how to walk through this time in our life.

Gradually most of the people who once shared meals with us and sat chatting on our couch, no longer phoned or visited. We had been given the space we needed to sort out our thoughts about Carl's condition. But the space was going on so much longer than we needed or wanted. On lonely weekend afternoons we talked about how we missed some of our friends and why they were no longer in touch.

Carl and I both remembered a neighbour named Lizzie who lived on the farm next door to his parents. Lizzie could not read or write but her eyes sparkled with life and her words with wisdom: "Everybody has their own struggles," she said often. Were these *disappeared* having struggles of their own?

I thought a lot about the way we form and keep friendships. I wrote in my journal: 'I have had expectations of others when they needed to be let go.' Eventually I stopped thinking and let my heart make the decision. The Cathys and Ruths of the world offer compassion and still keep us looking forward to the possibilities in our lives. That's what we needed right then. Maybe it's what everyone needs.

It's Not Brain Surgery... Or Is It?

As we began to understand more of what Carl's diagnosis meant, we propped one another up emotionally. Most of the time, while one of us fell apart, the other one was able to act normal, and this was very comforting. We were *all right so far*.

Retreating to the meadow or down to the lake I turned to my journals for consolation. The autumn winds whipped water into waves and I confided in my journal fears for Carl and doubts about my own ability to cope: 'The feeling is panic, and I want to run, not away and not to, just run. Maybe this would be to keep my mind on where my feet are, instead of where my heart is.'

One thing became clear: our lives needed simplifying. Music was what we had done when we were healthy. The commitment part of that felt unmanageable now. I gave up teaching piano lessons, and Carl and I gathered our musical friends together for some decision-making. The performing group *Double Vision* sang both sacred and secular music. Its unwritten goals were to do both music and community building, and to reach out to others and support those in the group. We had shared a lot of laughter over the past few years but it was time to disband.

When the nurses in the group wept quietly we knew they understood, probably far better than us, what we were facing. There was a sense of loss, but more palpable was the sense of resignation. We were doing what we needed to do for one another. I have read that there are only two questions one asks at the end of life: "Was I loved?" and "Was I loving?" We were releasing one another for what we needed right then, and we were doing it with love.

By now we had a name for Carl's condition: Arterial Vascular Malformation. As I understood it, the offending vessel pressed against the brainstem, making surgical intervention dangerous. Our initial shock past, we were beginning to have questions: *Could the doctors predict what symptoms would appear and at what speed?*

Already, Carl's bladder had shut down on a couple of occasions and there had been some visual disturbances. He was having increasing difficulty swallowing. But were all or any of these symptoms related to the brain? A friend let us know of a technique being used in cancer treatments, a non-invasive procedure called a gamma knife. *Might this gamma knife be any help? Was it being used in Canada?*

Carl's feeling of being trapped was manifesting itself in nightmares. It would help to have more information. It was the only kind of control he could have. He made a second trip to Toronto Western. We had until Christmas, they told us, to live normally. An angiogram and second MRI would follow. Based on what they found, we might expect surgery soon. Brain surgery. One at a time we dove into a tailspin. "What if," we asked ourselves, "what if ... ?" I tried to remain calm as Carl agonized over the unknown future. Once he regained control, it was my turn to lie on the bed, eyes shut, my imagination three scary steps ahead of my understanding, while Carl reminded me to stay in the here and now.

As long as we took turns falling apart, stress levels could be managed. But our life felt like a full teacup. One more drop of stress might cause it to spill over. Carl's Dad was now fighting pneumonia in Wiarton hospital. Katie, Carl's mother, needed our support, but the turmoil in our own lives had drained our emotional reserves. Something had to give, and we stopped *taking turns*, both of us down-spiraling at the same time. Communications weakened. Together-time disappeared.

I wanted to talk it all out. Talking reassured me. But Carl was in full denial. He shoved down his questions, his worries, and even his feelings. At home he alternately dozed and watched TV. This was a backwards step to a previous habit, I thought. His body was present but it seemed as if his mind was not. I hated watching him stare fixedly at the television screen, hour by hour. I too went backwards, withdrawing to the far end of the house with some music I liked and a library book. The air was cold there, far from the wood stove, but I huddled in the wicker rocking chair sinking into my own thoughts.

When after a few days we gathered the strength to talk things over, an uncomfortable realization crept over me. I had been struggling to make myself feel safe, and in doing that, I did not always choose my words carefully. If ever there was a time to see negative feelings for what they were, and choose words with consciousness, this was it. I was disappointed in my lack of insight during that difficult week. I felt ashamed to have been so focused on myself rather than on Carl.

It was time to take control of my life in so far as I could. I resolved to get information regarding insurance, and to notice things Carl could do now, but which he might be unable to do in future. I told myself that I must get into better physical shape. Those things were possible for me to do. I decided to let go of seeing it as my duty to keep everyone informed. It would be better to give my attention to spending quality time with others. Hardest to face was the fact that some of Carl's choices might not make sense to me, but he and I were different people. I must respect that his choices came out of his needs.

I wrote down a prayer in my journal: 'Let me live in the here and now, using my time to deepen connections. Let me be steady for others and grant me the strength to walk the road ahead. Let Light enter the fearful places.' There were enough of those ... fearful places.

This Is the One

Carl's symptoms were no worse but in our concerns over health we had almost lost track of Catherine and Stuart's wedding date just a few months away. Some mother and daughter time offered a welcome distraction.

Catherine must have thought "who better to take shopping for the most expensive dress you have ever bought, will ever buy, in your life?" than her mother, a self-professed bargain shopper extraordinaire. Eleven years of real estate disaster had trained us how to live when money was short. By the time we extricated ourselves and our money from the house-which-never-sold, I knew all too well how to find a good buy.

Did we expect to see two-for-the-price-of-one wedding gowns? Did we have a half-off coupon to present? We were inexperienced wedding gown shoppers but Catherine had in her mind the kind of dress she was looking for. The first two places on our list weren't open yet, but in the third shop Catherine tried on four dresses, all lovely, two worth considering.

At this point we needed to say: "We're checking out two more places and might be back later." But the saleslady hauled out her big guns: "I know this one is a little beyond your price range," she warned us, "but might you like to try it on?" Catherine put the dress on and stood half surrounded by full length mirrors. From the front the dress was simple in design with the square neckline which Catherine and I both favour. But it was the back of the dress I was looking at. The bodice laced up almost in medieval style and an overskirt could be gathered up or let down to the floor.

Did we ask if tax was included? No. Did we ask what alterations might cost? No. Were we calm and collected, nicely thanking the lady for her help while we moved on to see what other stores had to offer?

No. "This is the one! This is the one!" we exclaimed, just the way all those other mothers and daughters have done before us. But I have to tell you: the dress was beautiful.

For the next months Catherine would show us candleholders and trailing ivy plants. She would educate us in the kinds and colours of roses. Her small apartment dining room filled up with candles and vases and she took us shopping to make sure her Dad would have a good suit jacket and I would wear appropriate shoes.

"I don't want to dress fancy," I had complained. I hired a knitter to make a pretty little sweater jacket. A great success. Then I hired a seamstress (well, I thought she was a seamstress) to make a long skirt. I took it from my closet to show friends. They shook their heads sadly: "Sheila, you can't wear that to your daughter's wedding." It looked like a costume for a classroom play.

Once again my daughter took me shopping and together we chose a long navy gown with a filmy wrap. "You can still wear the little sweater in the evening," Catherine urged. A lifetime ago I had not been able to afford a *real* wedding dress. Carl's cousin, skilled at all the domestic arts, altered the only evening gown I had ever worn. In all our years together, my husband had never seen me dressed in anything elegant. He was delighted with the dress so I was too.

The Dress

It's hanging in the closet now
Dark and slender and silky soft
More elegant than anything I ever owned
or even dreamed of wearing.
It whispers as I pass it
and beckons me to muse anew:
Maybe I am not as old as I thought I was.

This Is Your Brain

On a grey November morning behind the house Carl and Michael put up white Christmas lights on a slender evergreen. If I was writing at night I could see it shining outside my window, the only light in the forest. Something about that tree helped me to feel hope in the midst of the health worries surrounding us.

What holds us steady through the fearful times? Trust in the bigger picture if we can keep it in our grasp. Maintaining a feeling of normalcy amidst the uncertainty. And family and friends who keep in regular touch. I had to learn in moments when I was most frightened, not to run away as was my instinct, but to walk towards friends.

My own *walk* had begun about three years earlier. We were in our early days at the lake. Carl's legs had not yet weakened enough to cause concern. Life was good. Life was normal. And then, nearing the end of a Remembrance Day program at the school, *good* and *normal* suddenly shifted. I sat at the piano playing one of the many Peace songs I had taught the children. I was young in the sixties after all, and I knew them all: *Bridge Over Troubled Water, We Shall Overcome, One Man's Hands* ...

But one woman's hand, my left hand to be exact, was not working. It was alive with a strange tingling, and I knew instinctively that something was terribly wrong. I stared at my hand and willed it to keep moving. The song finished and the assembly ended. I stood up. My grade five students would automatically rise and follow the class seated behind them. They were mature enough to get back to the classroom on their own. But I would need help. I started to move in what felt like slow motion towards my friend Lynn. Shouldn't I say something? I could not think what that might be but just looked full into her eyes. Quietly she walked towards me, concern shadowing her face, and led me out of the gym.

I sat in the principal's office like a misbehaved pupil. Word finally came that my doctor would see me right after lunch. "You're looking pretty flushed," the secretary said. "Go into the girls' washroom and look in the mirror." Other than the tingling in my left arm I felt fine, but trotted obediently across the hall to peek at my reflection. Flushed for sure. Red in fact. I should have been concerned but what I felt was curiosity. "Isn't that interesting!"

Back in the office, the principal Peter and I disagreed about next steps. "I'll drive you to the doctor's," he said. But whatever had been wrong appeared to be over now, red face or not. "I'll just drive up to my mother's," I insisted, "and when it's time I can get to the doctor's from there. It isn't far." Clearly reluctant, Peter let me go, but followed me in his car to be sure I reached my first destination safely.

Convincing the doctor that I could drive was not as easy. "You won't be doing any driving for a while," he told me. "I'm pretty sure you've had a stroke. We'll call Carl to come and get you, and we'll make an appointment in London."

While we waited for the London appointment, a carotid Doppler test was done at our local hospital. The medical technician had been pleasant and chatty. She found no cause for my stroke. My family doctor was not impressed. "This is your brain," he scolded. "We need to find out what happened."

The atmosphere at the London stroke clinic felt tense and the technician doing the test was silent. Not a word for twenty minutes as she passed the wand over my neck and throat. Her boss was only a little more talkative. His questions were brief and only once did he show any interest in my answers. When I mentioned that my arm still tingled when I took a bath, he seemed quite pleased. He did not share with me the source of his pleasure.

"Plan on a strict diet from now on," he informed me: "If it walks, swims, or flies, you eat only a tiny amount once a week." On the way out his receptionist said that I could have an egg once a year ... on my birthday. I followed these directions for about six weeks before telling my own doctor who laughed. "Oh for heaven's sake, just eat reasonably," he said. And it must have worked because a later CT scan showed all signs of the original stroke had disappeared.

All Right So Far

Three years after my stroke, the tingling in my left arm was just a memory. Now it was my inner being which trembled, as I grieved for Carl's disappearing health. Daily I watched my once strong husband crumbling slowly under the weight of the tiniest of blood vessels placed so insidiously against his brain stem. Sometimes the things you think you need to fear only mask the real dangers.

Traditions

There is something reassuring about traditions. If we are doing the same things we did pre-diagnosis, then maybe we are okay. So we carried on with our family's custom of attending the local museum's Christmas celebration.

The night was cold but inside light and music from the Salvation Army band had everyone smiling. Two young men with tweed caps and suspenders entered the room and the audience all but held its breath. This was what we were all waiting for. With great care, the men began lighting candles on the tall Christmas tree, long tapers in one hand and fire extinguishers in the other. *O Christmas Tree, O Christmas Tree* the band played, and we filed out the door. We passed an 1800's dining room re-creation. Each year the toys in the display were exactly the same. And each year my mother pointed out things she remembered from her childhood.

A short walk took us to the first little cabin and we crowded in, thinking about the pioneers and their primitive living conditions. How hard those beds must have been, and how cold, despite the flames in the huge open fireplace. The musician playing *God Rest Ye Merry, Gentlemen* was probably not expecting an outburst of four part harmony to accompany him, but where there is music our family cannot resist singing. Women in long cotton dresses and white house caps served out cups of goose stew to take out of the cabin.

The little building could hold only a dozen people at a time. So those coming in and those going out took turns at the narrow doorway and in a few minutes we stood by the open fire outside, solemnly spooning the steaming mixture into our mouths. I especially liked going to the log house just up the road. In its kitchen we chose fancy cookies to go with our apple cider. A swag of fat-bellied calico gingerbread men with ribbons at their necks hung in one window. I looked for it every year.

Outdoors we waited for the horse drawn sleigh to pass by. "The plum pudding is my favourite," Catherine told us while we walked up the snowy road to the 1930's house. Soon we were eating the plum pudding on the back porch. This reminded Carl and me that our own Christmas cakes still needed to be put together the next morning.

My Christmas cake recipe came to me from a family at Bayview School where I taught for most of my career. Three brothers ended up in my home room in consecutive years, and each year at Christmas the brother I happened to be teaching at the time brought me one of their mother's delicious Christmas cakes. It was the best fruitcake I had ever tasted and I told the boys so, especially lamenting to David the youngest of the three that since there were no brothers left I would never taste his mother's wonderful cake again. That June, I was on yard duty when David slipped up behind me: "Check your desk after recess," he suggested, "I think Santa might have been here." Sure enough, there on my desk was the recipe with *Ho Ho Ho* printed on the envelope. I still keep that tattered envelope in the back of a favourite cookbook.

Carl always mixed the fruit for the cake at night so the flavours would meld together before morning. We had substituted extra cherries for the mixed peel, and I had done my confused-woman-in-wine-shop routine. I never knew what kind of wine to buy, and the brands appeared to change from year to year. Male clerks found me and my wine search perplexing, but if I could find a female clerk she always seemed to understand, grabbing a bottle off the shelf in business like manner: "This is what you need."

In the morning I cut and greased both sides of brown paper strips to line the glass loaf pans while Carl spooned out generous portions of last night's batter from the large roasting pan. We put the cakes into the oven with a pan of water, not really knowing why other than we had always done it that way. It was good that the cake was made, because although December was upon us, it was our only Christmas preparation so far. Sending out cards, decorating, and wrapping gifts lost all appeal and loomed over me like a threat. Carl's health took most of our attention.

I felt unsettled much of the time and wondered how best to relax. I bought a yoga tape to see if the old familiar exercises might help but instead my mind wandered and I kept looking at the clock to see how long I had lasted. I was tense. Would a different approach help? I remembered reading a piece of wisdom which made a lot of sense: 'There are only two things worth getting anxious about: Life and how we live it, death and how we meet it.'

In my journal I wrote: My pre-occupation with Carl's health and what will happen to him and to the kids and I, has changed me in some ways. I see myself living less in the here and now than is good, or even healthy, for me. My physical health is also weak after my recent bout of bronchitis. I feel as if I'm not giving enough to anybody: myself, my husband, my children.

In my anxiety I had been concentrating on what I might be losing, instead of what I could accept or adjust. Nothing good could come from such negative thinking. I decided to get back to writing down things I was grateful for: the beautiful winter skies on an afternoon drive with Michael, loving letters from friends, extra kindnesses shown by other staff members at the church. Even having Carl come in the door with a pizza felt like cause for celebration.

There is nothing like darkness to make the light stand out more clearly. I was never a Bob Dylan fan, but I sure agreed with his words: 'If we're not busy being born, we're busy dying.' Deep inside, I knew it was high time Carl and I get busy being born. Being born is not easy. It takes work. If we were to revive our ailing marriage, we would need to spend time as a couple rediscovering things we liked to do together. Where was our retirement? I felt cheated, barely understanding that work was Carl's therapy. I hoped the holiday season would interrupt the cycle of his self-imposed sixty hour work weeks and give me my husband's company back.

Family would be coming for some time together soon and everyone could use a distraction. So I drew a huge Christmas tree on newspaper and asked Carl to transfer it to plywood. We painted it and attached paper ornaments with instructions such as: *describe any room or piece of furniture in your first home*, or *give a memory from your school days*.

The tree was about three feet high, but it lay flat, a board game, but a rather large one. We made up *Bognor cards*, from the family's terrible real estate experiment: *your tenant's dogs have dug two large holes in the back yard. Go back one space.*

The day came to try out the game and we crowded into the living room, pretty nieces in a tangle of arms and legs lounging on the couch, dining room and rocking chairs pulled into a wider circle to include everybody. We had each chosen a small symbol to represent us as it jumped around the board. There were tiny cat and owl figurines, thimbles, bells, measuring tapes … much more fun than traditional game figures, we thought. Rolling dice, we jumped our symbols around the tree ornaments: *tell us about a place you went with your family as a child.*

When someone reached the top of the tree they were allowed to choose a gift. Guys had brought guy-gifts, and girls had brought girl-gifts. Both groups were mystified at the choices made by the opposite sex. The women's eyes widened at the sight of their men overjoyed at receiving small tools. The men shook their heads over yet one more jar of bubble bath.

Christmas Eve day arrived before we managed a flurry of final house tidying and wrapping the gifts. The pageant that night went pretty well. With children scarce in this church, adults filled in as needed, giving us three generations of shepherds and angels. Knowing Michael and Carl were in the sound booth helping with the lighting made me happy. As the last notes of *Silent Night* drifted away, people blew out their candles, the lights came on full, and with a sense of real joy and with every jazz chord I knew, I played my traditional welcome to Christmas: *Rise Up Shepherd and Follow.*

Last Leg of the Journey

Friends whose kids lived on either coast would consider us well off, but the two and a half hour drive home from Guelph always seemed long to me. If we were lucky on such trips the car radio would pick up the Toronto jazz station for the first hour. Most often we talked. Like most married couples we talked over what might be happening in the week ahead, or whether the dishwasher needed replacing or when we should have friends over for dinner. And sometimes, the talk became more serious as it did that Boxing Day.

The holiday had inserted a spoke in the wheel of our dwindling connection to one another. For days now we had lived more like the old us instead of Carl sleeping on the couch by the wood stove and me huddled in the rocker at the far end of the house. But we were driving home to the pre-Christmas life in which our tightly knit marriage had been unraveling. Was the distance between us simply an unavoidable product of not spending enough time together? Could we (should we) try to get back to who we had once been as a couple? Or were we changing too much as individuals to continue together?

We turned east. Last leg of the journey. "What do you need to make you feel happy?" I asked Carl. He didn't like thinking about questions like this, but I was determined to explore issues which had troubled me for a long time. I waited, mentally counting to ten. I didn't want to let him off the hook by filling in the gap in conversation even though I knew this was what he would rather have happen.

After what seemed a long time he replied: "I don't know." He did know. I knew he did. My persistence was not from any true need to get an answer. By now I knew well that being *plaid* as he called it, being out in the world feeling useful was what made him feel happy after thirty-five years in the classroom. We had talked about this *plaid versus professional* issue often enough in the past. "But you were useful," I always insisted.

"How more useful could a person be than to change young lives?" Still, as I well knew, Carl wanted to work with his hands, T-shirts and plaid flannel a sort of uniform.

Leading him to talk was my way of getting him to think about the subject of happiness. Hopefully mine as well as his own. I rolled the car window down a crack waiting for him to continue. He stared across the steering wheel in silence. Through the Christmas season we had spent more time together, as we had in our *pre-plaid* life. I had so needed that time together. Now I needed him to tell me our marriage still mattered to him. I tried again coming at it from a new direction: "Why do you think we're together?"

Carl might well be uncomfortable. But having found an opportunity to address troubling topics, I held on like a bulldog: "I think we choose our partners in order to teach and learn the lessons of life. What lessons do you think we've been learning in these past two difficult years?" (*Please let him see how we have spent less and less time together, how his driven personality and my feelings of abandonment are widening the gap between us.*) Carl remained silent, staring at the road in front of the car. "Could your brain disorder be a gigantic wake-up call from the Universe?"

These questions had been in my mind for a long while. I had reached the point where I wanted the return of the old Carl or some reasonable facsimile. But Carl was not in the same place emotionally. He had denied all along that our relationship was strained. His good health appeared lost. *Was he now to lose his wife as well?*

I was taken by surprise when his response to my questions was anger. A few minutes from home he abruptly stopped the car on the snowy road, wrenched off his seat belt, shoved open the door and stomped off into the black night. If my questions were threatening to him, this behaviour was equally threatening to me. Indignant, I climbed behind the wheel and sped off, but only as far as the next side road where I shut off the engine and sat, mind racing. I knew I had been pushing him, but I was determined that if I was going to stay in this marriage we must work through this. After a few minutes of cooling down, I picked him up and we drove home in an ill at ease truce. "I'll give it a year," I told him. "If we can't 'fix it' in a year, I can't see staying together."

Ready to Bargain

The next few days were like no other time in our marriage. We were polite but quiet. I avoided Carl's eyes. I could not look in case I might see there, a future I did not want to see. Carl's mind had snapped to attention. He was finally getting it. "She's really going to leave." He knew and I knew that he knew. This was enough incentive for us to begin reassembling the bits of our relationship. Carl now understood that I would not live in a disconnected marriage forever. I had finally taken a stand, even if the deadline I had given was pulled from thin air. How could I possibly know where we would be a year from now? There could not be a timetable for making things right again.

At first we danced cautiously around one another, talking about anything but the blow-up and the underlying reasons for it. Finally, on the last day of the year the distance between us was too much for either of us to bear. We set our pain aside. Almost shyly we reached out to hold one another. I lay my head against Carl's shoulder feeling his arms wrap around me. Touch reconnected us and we remembered at heart level who we were. How often do couples detach and not find their way back to one another? We knew this was just a beginning. We had no idea how much emotional work lay ahead of us. But the healing had begun.

I puttered around the kitchen the following day. New Year's day or not, Carl had places to go and people to work for. For a change, his absence felt okay to me, giving me space to think about the reattachment of our broken marriage. But why did I not feel more peaceful? Instead I was falling to pieces. Everything made me cry. In the midst of this emotional storm, Cathy phoned. Sensing my incoherent state she offered what help she could. "Just listen to me talk and don't feel you need to say anything yourself," she advised. I assured her I would be fine, and continued cooking and crying until by late afternoon, when Carl returned from work, the storm had passed.

My strongest intention at this start of a new year was to deepen connections with family and friends, my husband being at the top of that list. Our marriage was tottering forward once more but on shaky feet. And Carl and I still had to find our way through the fear we were facing concerning his health. I hated the large role anxiety was playing in our life and asked in my journal: *Is it enough to be safe for now?*

In many ways I felt like a child huddled beneath the cloak of *normal*, sitting in the only safe spot she had ever known ... her marriage. But how long would it remain safe? When Carl's brain condition had been diagnosed, the doctor had heard of only one other case. Since that time, we had been told there were three cases in North America but that one of the patients had died. Although we had not been given any kind of prognosis or time line, it felt to Carl like an anvil hanging over his head.

Around this time an upsetting dream haunted me. I saw myself in a car with a group of women, all younger and stronger than me. We were heading home from a distance. By the roadside I spotted a favourite sweater of mine, and I wanted to stop and get it. They told me that sadly, this would not be possible. "But it cost a lot," I told them, "and I treasure it dearly. I have taken such good care of it." Gently they explained that someone else would now take care of it, although perhaps I could retrieve it later. I was very sad, as I thought that was unlikely to happen.

I wrote in my journal that I was afraid the sweater in my dream represented Carl. *Indeed I have treasured and taken care of him, and I don't want to go home without him.*

The dream set off two or three days of frequent weeping. I turned to the computer and my worry and uncertainty poured onto the page:

I'm ready to bargain now God. I didn't understand before.
I knew it in my head of course,
But my heart was blind and deaf and most of all dumb.
And now it wants to make a deal.
"I'll love him better than before if you will spare him."
All that talk about accepting the bigger picture?
That was just my head, God. I need you to listen to my heart.

Catherine must have been alarmed by the sadness, which seeped through our telephone conversations. Her decision to come home for a few days brightened our spirits like nothing else could have. While we waited for her visit I consciously looked for comforting activities. Often I set out candles to make the house feel warm and welcoming. I enjoyed warm baths and spent hours writing and baking. There were old photo albums to look through and always music, whether playing piano or listening to any of our collection of CDs. Looking back on it later, I would think: *what luxury to have all that time to do happy things*.

I had a good talk with some friends about how I was dealing with the emotional side of things. "I'm crying a lot," I confessed, "instead of dealing with it." One of the women answered firmly that I needn't think of crying as "not dealing with it" ... but rather see how crying was just one of the ways we were getting through it. This helped as I sometimes felt like I was being *weak* when I had those weepy days.

To celebrate having Catherine home, we cooked a special meal to eat in candlelight. We have always liked music with our meals so Charlotte Church's beautiful voice rang through the house and we set out rarely used plates my godmother gave me many years ago. The date 1933 is engraved on the backs of the dishes which have edges circled by gold vines on a royal blue background. Orange and yellow flowers are placed at intervals against the blue border. I marvel at such lovely dishes once being handed out as prizes at the movie theater, but my mother told me more than once this is where Aunt Ivy first obtained the plates. I am careful with them, rarely using them, but having both our children with us at the table was a rare treat.

The next evening, Michael and Catherine returned from visiting their grandmother and came to sit and chat in our bedroom. We talked about their visit with Katie as the little electric stove warmed the space and our four window candles made the room glow rose-coloured. We didn't talk about Carl's health. This was a subject any two of us might discuss but for some reason, talking about it as a family felt too strange.

A day or two later Catherine left for Guelph. I gathered my strength to make phone calls of a practical nature. What kind of insurance coverage did we have? How were our small RRSP's set up? Was Carl's pension life-insured? It felt so callous asking such things, and yet it seemed wiser not to keep pushing it aside. Carl believed he was dying so I believed it too.

Brenda, a friend since childhood, wrote to advise: "Take one day at a time so as not to get too overwhelmed. It is not always easy to let go if one is of strong and independent character as I know you two possess." She included a lovely prayer. Though I don't know where the actual prayer came from, the first line is often used in readings at funeral services:

Let not your hearts be troubled.
I'll take care of the burden.
Don't give it a thought. Leave it to me.

Could I do that? Could I let go of the worries and live with a peaceful heart?

Dancing in the Dark

We had found our way through a variety of storms this winter but bad times remind us what is really important and propel us to cling to one another.

For many months Grandpa had been a soul trapped in a body which did not work very well. In a matter of weeks Carl became patient in one part of his life and caregiver in another, shaving his father's face as he lay in a hospital bed. Weeks earlier at Christmas we had bought Grandpa, who had always liked gadgets, a jelly-bean machine. I played carols on the piano, and we ate a meal together, but it was hard to maintain any degree of vibrancy, and even the small yellow bird in his corner cage looked neglected and forlorn. It did not feel like Christmas to us, and probably not to Carl's Dad either.

In his months at the home he had tried to communicate with us. "Two of them," he would say, but exactly what there were two of was beyond our understanding. It was also hard to know how much of our conversation he comprehended. He nodded a lot to show that he understood, or wanted to understand. We kept our visits short, partly for Grandpa's sake, and partly for our own.

Early one morning while we slept, Grandpa passed away. The family gathered at Katie's and spread out photos on the living room floor. We talked about how Carl's Dad had loved his vehicles, the cars and especially the snowmobiles, which he had always made available to kids and grandkids for tearing around the farm. We laughed about how he liked to cook baked beans and in a fit of silliness we decided to put his recipe on the funeral card. Silly or not, a lot of people asked for the card strictly because of that recipe. The funeral home ran out and had to print more.

We wrote a eulogy, Carl searching his memory to go beyond recent years to find a father who loved to fix things, and long ago taught his son to fly kites. I did not have those childhood memories to fall back on. To me Carl's father was the man who sat on my left at their big kitchen table, firmly anchored into place as if to ground his wife who jumped from her seat every few minutes to fill a bowl or fetch something from the cupboard, constantly accompanied by a chorus of "For heaven's sake, Katie, sit down and eat."

Twenty-five years ago I had wondered what to call my new in-laws. Carl's Mom became Katie, as she was to everyone. But I could never bring myself to address Carl's father as Stewart, and though my own father had been gone since I was a young teenager, this man could not be Dad to me. He treated me with a slight formality, insisting through hundreds of meals over the years that I serve myself first before passing him the food. It was our little ritual. I picked up the mashed potatoes and held them out to him and he nodded his head pointing at my plate.

Time with my own father had been short. But I remembered sitting on his knee for stories and songs, happily greeting him as he unpacked his railroader's lunch pail, standing by his chair math book in hand saying "Oh now I get it!" to his patient reading of instructions previously judged impossible in my panic-blocked mind. In terms of years, I had known Grandpa twice as long as I had known my own father. But how much did I really know this man in suspenders and plaid shirt, waiting for me to serve my plate first?

Carl knew him in the field throwing bales of hay onto wagons. He knew him in the barn mucking out stalls. He knew him in the back shed fixing yet another piece of equipment, maybe the place he was happiest. Here was another ability he passed on, not with direct teaching so was it in the genes? Our Michael, Stewart's only grandson, sometimes said "In pioneer times I would have been a tinker." And Carl did his share of tinkering as well, mostly from financial necessity, but probably following his father's example.

Our relationship was beginning to feel more peaceful. I thought a lot about change and what it meant in our lives. I tried not to think too much about specific changes we might be facing, because truly, nobody knew what those would be. "I am in waiting mode," I wrote in my journal, "but this thinking about what might happen is living outside the here and now, and spending energy unnecessarily. I know in my heart that the words *now is all we ever have*, are true".

Grandpa dreamed of big changes once. We knew nothing of this until after his death when a relative told how as a young man Stewart had been offered the chance of a job in the States. It was a fixing/tinkering kind of job, easier than working on the farm, appealing to a man who preferred workshop to barn. He wanted that job but there was the farm to look after, complete with aging mother. He stayed with the land. He stayed with the family.

Dancing in the Dark

In its kinder moments
Life slow-dances us 'round the edges of the room,
Bending us, blending us,
Until, absorbed into the surroundings,
We disappear in the turns and intimacy and familiar faces that line
the fringes.
And we try to take it all in
And we want to shut out the insistent whispers
That any moment now the tune will change to a wild tango
and, caught in the center of it all
we won't know the steps and we won't like the song
and we'll want to run wild-eyed from the dance-floor. (I never knew
it would be like this how could you bring me here).
But Life whispers in our ear: They're still playing our song!
Just listen to the music. That's all you need to do.

Candles in the Window

Winter is such a dark time. We have to make light where we can. "No Christmas lights up before Remembrance Day" has long been my policy, but in a way I understand why so many people put their lights on early and keep them up late. We all look for light in a Canadian winter. One dark winter evening though, I drove into the yard and noticed far more light than seemed normal. A warm but curious glow surrounded the house. I gathered purse and packages and climbed out of the car to walk in the door and discover every string of white mini-lights we owned, lighting up the sitting room. Carl was testing them before lending them out for a float in the Christmas parade.

In our bedroom windows facing the road we kept four candles as a lighting-the-way-through-the-forest tradition to welcome guests. Once in a while I lit them for my own pleasure and walked down the road just so I could walk back to the house looking at them. More often Carl and I lit them for one another. Stopping the car at the outer gate I would see the lights ahead and know my husband was looking forward to my return.

When I arrived home one evening, Abby was sitting in the window, rose colored walls shining softly behind her. Of all the moments in my life, this was one in which I would have chosen to be an artist I could have captured that moment in a painting.

One night I dreamed about being unable to see the road ahead. In the dream, a winter moon lit the forest and I searched for the road buried beneath a blanket of snow. Carl had taken the other direction, accompanied by loved ones and I peered through the darkness trying to discern the lights of home. Only two of our candles were visible and even these showed only at brief moments. I could not see the road, but could I feel where it lay beneath my feet?

Clearly, my fears of an unknown future and worry that Carl might die were creeping into my dreams. Already he had to struggle hard to get to his feet from a sitting or lying down position. Most frightening were those times when he was suddenly unable to swallow. Lying on the bed together watching a TV program I would sense Carl's body tense up. I put a hand on his arm and talked softly waiting for him to get control. I could hardly imagine how frightening this must feel. For many people walking is painful, but Carl faced a double threat. In addition to the brainstem anomaly, serious knee problems meant that walking was no longer an automatic function. At each step, he needed to think about lifting and placing his feet. He staggered and stumbled more, and falling was an ever present danger. Most distressing were those days when Carl had no control of his legs upon waking. Some mornings he had to crawl to the bathroom. "I pull myself along the floor using my hands and my arms, and dragging my body from the waist down," he explained, "and I don't want you there to watch."

We slept in separate rooms. He could call me if need be. But mostly what he needed was for me not to see what he regarded as a humiliating circumstance. His life was full of loss, but embarrassment hurt most of all. One day, trying to pile wood, he fell and could not get up. Michael said later, "Mom, I wanted to help him, but it seemed better to pretend I hadn't seen." Other people would never understand this, but I knew Michael had made the right call. He looked away as his father needed him to. It may seem strange for a wife and son to ignore a loved one in such distressing circumstances. But when all you can do is not look, then you do it. Sometimes the *lost* ability seemed worse than it really was.

Carl somehow adapted, learning what he must do differently. In a period of weeks he adjusted to the swallowing problems so that he didn't become panicky any longer. The difficulty in rising from a sitting position was permanent. And Carl came to understand that he had to move very slowly upon waking, but that concentration would then let him walk.

Whenever a lost capability has not come back we have tried to keep in mind the plateaus between losses. One step down. Adjust,

Another step. Adjust again. In front of us the road lies hidden. We just have to feel our way through the dark places and trust there will be candles in the window.

Breathing Room

Often I grappled with the role I thought of as 'Suzy Homemaker'. I could settle into a rocking chair for an hour to sew missing buttons back onto shirts or spend an occasional morning in the kitchen cooking. The radio kept me company by the kitchen window while I cracked eggs open with a butter knife, and mashed shortening and sugar together with a big spoon. 'Suzy Homemaker' is part of my heritage. I picture my mother in a clean cotton blouse standing at her ironing board on a hot summer day, a 7-Up close at hand with the straw sticking out of the bottle.

But I have never been my mother. Much as I might try to be fully in the domestic moment, turning on CBC radio to keep me company, other activities soon lure me away. Housekeeping has never been a focal point in my life. For me it is do the laundry, get the groceries, meet acceptable standards of cleanliness, and try to get some kind of control over the clutter. That's it. I can admire the beautifully kept houses of other people. I can understand how living in such order could bring a sense of peace. I'm just not there yet, if there is a place I will ever want or manage to be.

I remember a strongly feminist friend helping me pack boxes of books one day and gasping over the advice in a paperback which insisted that women are to go out of their way to welcome their Man home at the end of the day. But I have never seen.... I have never seen that kind of behaviour, or the sewing of buttons or baking of cookies as being incompatible with being a strong modern woman. Over the years I always liked welcoming my man home. I was glad to see him. I had much to share. It was not uncommon in our home for me to put on a little makeup, choose some relaxing music, and light the candles in the windows when Carl was away. Whether for husband or friends or just for myself, I have always wanted the mood to be warm and welcoming. And besides, you can hardly even see dust-bunnies by candlelight. But that is as far as I go towards being 'Suzy Homemaker'.

And Carl. Who is he? Even with his health in clear decline, he remained determined to carry on, to go out into the community and to prove to himself that he still has something to offer. Many times I've pleaded with him to accept that family, friends, and even acquaintances, valued him for his vibrant self ... for who he was, not what he could do. He could not see that. "Just do it," had been his motto. In a fit of silliness he once exclaimed "All I was doing was being." The truth of those words tore through me like lightning. But while he said the words, he appeared not to believe them. He felt driven to accomplish something. *Being* must wait in the wings when *doing* takes on so much importance.

Strong the Dancer

"I want to be remembered," he cries, "For strength and capability."
And I'll grant him that. He was strong.
He threw mind and body hard at each new problem.
And delighted in the solving. And yes, he was strong.
But does he not see? It is not his strength and capability we most looked up to.
The weight that muscles once could carry was nothing to the weight his heart bears now.

To us, he was, and is, and will be still Builder of boats and Flyer of kites,
Bright figure dancing on the dark stage. Music in his soul. Joy in his heart.
There are other ways to dance, dear soul, dear heart. It is time to learn them.
There are new strengths, Not in the dancer, but in the dance itself.

Telling Carl to find a new identity was one thing. Finding my own new dance was another. Talk about the pot calling the kettle black! I had worn the *Carl's wife and friend* identity so long, I hardly remembered who to be me on my own. "We are no longer out in the world together," I wrote in my journal. "My world has shrunk considerably so that I spend almost no time away from home."

Drawing into my own home made me pull somehow further into myself. I recognized that it had to do with feeling safe. "I have not found a way to be in the world by myself," I wrote. "I liked being half of a couple who were making a difference with family, and friends, and in the community. That defined who I was, and now sometimes, I feel like nobody. How much I have given up. How different this stage of life is from what I imagined it would be."

It was time to 'talk tough' to the discouraged part of me. But talking to that part of me was one thing. Having it pay attention was quite another. I wrote some advice to myself:

> 1. Do not wait to be chosen. Choose.
> 2. Being taken care of is not the same as being loved. Stand strong on your own.
> 3. Challenge inertia regarding *have to's*, and balance these things out with *want to's*.

When Carl and I chose to spend our life together it was not so that two of us could make one whole. I had always felt that each of us was complete already. So how did I get to a place where I saw myself as *not enough*? How did Carl get to a place where being useful had taken on more importance than being loved or loving? Mornings when Carl left I headed, still in nightgown, to the computer, words spilling over one another in my mind. Writing the words down helped. But I needed most of all to have Carl see what I was feeling. Many days he would come home to find a poem on his pillow.

Breathing Room

*Since when does absence
make the heart grow fonder?
Oh the tiny absences perhaps,
creating little spaces in the structure of the marriage,
perhaps they let you see out,
perhaps they let some air in.
But when the structure itself is made more of absence than presence,
the holes are wide and widening until they join into one big hole
and you can see out fine because the structure is gone
and there is more air than you ever craved
and you can breathe it all (if you want to).*

*The shelter of course is gone.
The safe place you built together
out of shared memories and experiences,
walls constructed over years
ceilings painted with love to withstand the rain and the tears.
And now you sit in the empty space
clutching your hammer and your saw
wondering why you cannot form a foundation out of air,
re-connect the holes into walls
cover it all with a roof of happiness.*

Fragments and Remnants

"This is not the way I expected our retirement to be." Dissatisfied with the season outdoors and this particular season in my life, the season-of-the-absent-husband, I grumbled inwardly. Then I scolded myself for being negative when there was so much to be thankful for. I needed something to look forward to. The Olympics Opening Ceremonies were set for this Friday night. Why not prepare a beautiful supper and make the evening a celebration?

When Friday came I coated chicken pieces with crushed almonds, peeled and boiled beets, mashed potatoes and made a cheese sauce for the cauliflower. Carl and I shared the meal while we watched the opening ceremonies together. It was almost like a date. For the next few days my spirits lifted and then cabin fever asserted itself once more. I watched friend after friend go off each winter to faraway places. The little retirement holidays I had envisioned for so long had never, and between Carl's failing health and drive to keep working, *would* never, come about.

Talking to a friend one day I confided my feelings of shame "Imagine getting into this cellar of self-pity over something as small as a holiday," I lamented. My friend replied, "that in itself is a grieving process". This was just what I needed to hear as it was not helpful to me or anyone else, to feel bad about feeling bad. Carl's long work days continued, and I waited at home for a scrap of his remaining waking hours. It was a time of isolation.

I did my church work and the housework, and I checked on both Grandmas. I read, and wrote, and e-mailed everybody, keeping busy Monday to Friday. But it was my husband's company I wanted on this lonely Saturday afternoon, my mind running back and forth between feeling agitated and distraught, like a string of carnival ducks in a shooting gallery. By the time Carl came home I had emerged from the cellars of self-pity with a conclusion. I deserved — we both deserved, quality time together. If Carl could not see that, then I must at least salvage some sense of self-respect. I must stop begging him to keep a promise he had made short months ago, to spend one afternoon a week with me.

We sat on the bed together. I was releasing him from his promise, I explained. From now on, he did not need to spend any of his time with me. Over the last few months when words failed to show him how deserted I felt, I sometimes took a piece of paper and ripped off a corner, explaining that this was all I had left of him. The little paper had been getting smaller and smaller but still Carl didn't get my meaning. Now I tore off a tiny fragment from a page sitting on the bedside table. I handed him the fingernail sized scrap of paper and he stepped backwards in sudden, startled comprehension:

"I don't want to take it."

"Please take it. It's all I have left. I need to give it to you myself, not wait for it to be taken away. Leave me some little shred of dignity."

He took the sad little remnant. Both of us were weeping. "How did this happen?" he asked. He spoke of the changes in his personality and his behaviours over the past two years. He asked me to trust that he would give me back the often asked for piece of his time, an afternoon a week, which I needed, as much as a symbol that our marriage was still there, as for itself. Had I asked for too much? I didn't think so, but I couldn't get any perspective on the situation.

I woke in the night and propped pillows up on the bed. My journal was there on the bedside table and in the quiet room I wrote: "I must find the strength to put aside my own smaller loss, Carl's companionship, in the face of the losses he is coping with. I will weigh my words in the coming day. Carl should not need to worry about our relationship right now. Let me deepen the connection in whatever time we have, and stop begging for more time. I am not proud of where my focus was today. Let me do better tomorrow."

Remnants

I know it's up there high on a shelf:
The box of scraps left from our marriage.
Bright ones of happier times.
Soft ones of dreams discarded.
Small ones barely remembered,
Large ones full of promise.
Some sharp-edged,
Some gently rounded.
We cannot restore them to what they once were.
But if you'll help me reach up and ease it forward,
Perhaps we could lift it down together,
Explore the pieces,
Wondering at what once was,
Fashion some fresh-familiar thing from what is left.
Something different from what we had before.
Not altogether new, but a revisiting of memories.
A revival of dreams into a quilt.
Loved for its fragments of the past,
Needed for its promise to the future.
A quilt ... Even one of memories and dreams,
Can be crafted.

But quilts need time and attention.
They don't just happen.
They are loved into being.

Could we rebuild some of what we once had? Carl said sadly that he had 'forgotten how to be my husband' and it seemed to me that his drawing back from our marriage had run parallel with the decline in his health.

Medical tests were routine by now, along with trips to Toronto and what felt like endless waiting, not just for the tests themselves, but for results afterwards. With no word weeks after Carl had an angiogram we called down. Hospital staff checked their records to find he had been 'lost in the shuffle' and should come down for more tests in a few days time. It seemed to me 'lost in the shuffle' described perfectly, his health and our marriage.

Lessons

For a couple trying to nurse a bruised marriage, Valentine's Day seemed a good time to act. I wanted to remember the good times and I wanted Carl to remember them too. I searched through photo albums from the last thirty years, choosing pictures to produce a new album which would show who Carl was (at least in my eyes). I started with a picture of Carl striding purposefully out of the church on our wedding day, left hand closed over mine on his right arm, looking like he just won a prize.

The collection showed every aspect of our life over thirty years, Carl with his first boat, swimming with the children, arranging a bouquet for a flower show, cutting peoples' hair, pushing the soapbox racer he and Michael built. Here he was bent over in the garden, there splattered with paint in the house he built from the ground up. There were shots of Carl's stage sets for a big figure skating show, dinner plates decorated with nasturtium blossoms from the time we turned the dining room into a restaurant for a fund raising event.

One picture showed the ocean with a mist of spray above something black, a whale, though it was hard to tell, a memory shared by father and daughter from our only big vacation when Carl took Catherine whale watching. Further in the album a line of black wooden cats Carl had made lined the mantel while waiting to be given as Christmas gifts. Cartoon eyes stared out above long whiskers and bow ties, and against the brick of the fireplace stiff wooden tails stood at attention.

The album showed Carl with friend Marion looking over the edge of the bridge he built in memory of her husband Bud. There was Carl at the farm, Carl playing Santa, Carl feeding chipmunks. Carl lying on the bed reading with a cat lying on his back, Carl as quizmaster for a Trivia night.

On Valentine's Day, I watched my husband go through the little book, remembering. Fifty pictures spoke to him of the life he used to live, the man he used to be. Carl had his own surprise. He had gone to the florist's on the busiest day of her year and asked to use her flowers and her premises to put together a beautiful flower arrangement in the colours we had used for our wedding so many years ago. I was delighted with the pale pink carnations and baby's breath, but he only said, "look further." The grey pottery bowl holding the bouquet was one I had sorrowed over when it met with an accident months earlier breaking into two pieces. Carl had built it anew and covered the crack with something of beauty. I took it as a sign for our future.

Attending 'Canada Blooms', the huge flower show in Toronto, had been a rite of spring for us. Now in addition to Carl's difficulty walking he suffered complications following a mistake in his last hospital treatment. His bladder frequently shut down and a catheter was needed. So we gave up the thought of travel. Carl did not complain but anyone could see his sadness. Carl could not go to the flower show but could we bring a flower show to Carl? I could imagine written by an invisible hand on some gigantic cosmic shopping list: 'Buy hyacinths to feed his soul'.

> *If of thy mortal goods thou art bereft,*
> *And from thy slender store two loaves alone to thee are left,*
> *Sell one, and with the dole*
> *Buy hyacinths to feed thy soul.*
>   Thirteenth Century Persian Poet

At the grocery store my good-hearted neighbour, Ruth, helped me load a shopping cart with a bouquet of cut flowers, an azalea, mini-daffodils and a primula for spring, two gerbera daisies, one of them a sensational shade of red, and a hibiscus loaded with buds. At home, Michael and I placed flowers around the house and in each little corner where a plant stood, we lit a candle. The flowers which had seemed plentiful in the shopping cart were spread a bit far and thin in the family room. But Carl liked them anyway. Flowers had always brightened his world. It truly needed brightening at this time as he was very conscious of losing physical coordination and strength. Our own personal flower show in Moo Alley seemed a good way to end the winter.

Moo Alley was named by my brother, in honour of the neighbouring farmer's cattle, who passed by our yard daily and came right in to visit more often than we liked. The cattle were in residence from May until late fall, sometimes as late as the end of November.

In spring, thankfully cattle-free, Moo Alley became more like Moo Island. Though it only happened for a few days each year in late winter/early spring, huge puddles formed and we joked about living on 'A-River-Runs-Through-It-Road'. On a balmy spring day you could go out with a shovel and a long stick and be a child again, with the breeze riffling your hair while you dug little trenches and pretended that you and your shovel were making a difference. Late winter. Early spring. It reminded you that in death comes a birth.

Carl seemed to believe he was dying. Returning from a medical appointment, he would throw his jacket into the coat closet, sighing, and hold on to the closet frame with one hand, removing his shoes.

"But what did the doctor say, that has you so worried?"

He could not give me an answer. As far as I could tell, no big change had happened, at least physically. But he seemed troubled in his soul.

> Journal entry March 8/02:
> I do not know if I am watching Carl's spirit being born or dying. It seems like some of each. It feels only fair that if his strength of body must shut down, it should be replaced by a new strength of spirit. Certainly I am seeing labour pains as he struggles with his losses. At least, loss usually has gain as a flip side. So we lose things we liked to do when Carl's health was better. But we gain the extra love and support of friends. Hopefully, somewhere in that experience, we learn more about how to trust.

I worked for a while with Reverend George McPhee, who we called 'Toughlove George' behind his back. George came to the ministry late in life, large in body and in spirit, insightful and wise in his approach to people and their problems. In one Sunday sermon George told a wonderful story about trust. A snail is climbing up an apple tree in the dead of winter. A worm on a branch above looks down at the slow-moving snail and asks: "Are you crazy? There are no apples up there!" And the snail replies: "There will be when I get there." That is the kind of trust I want us to have. Trust that we have not yet seen the blossoms, let alone the fruit, but that they are there waiting, even in this dead of winter.

I awoke one night during a power outage and scribbled down some thoughts by candlelight: The next night, with power restored, I woke and wrote again. My insomniac musings, which happen several times a week, I refer to as my *nightwatch*.

> Journal entry March 11/02 Nightwatch:
>
> Outside my window the evergreen glows steadily at 3am, like a giant nightlight, its timer having been altered while the hydro was off. It seems on these cold dark days that I never know where the bright spots might come from: flowers at winter's end, lights shining in the dead of night.

The Inner Child is Out

O NE NIGHT WE HAD A FIGHT. Carl lay on his side of the bed. I sat on my side:

"Why do you have to shout?"

"Because you don't hear me unless I shout."

"I don't hear you *when* you shout. I lose all the meaning and only hear the anger."

Did we fight more than other couples? I have no way of measuring that. But our fights got shorter over the years. This one probably lasted an hour or so. Like so many arguments, once over we don't even remember what they were about. But what I do remember is that somewhere that night Carl seemed different ... more like his old self. He was giving again.

Somewhere in the middle of the squabble he calmed me and held me, and for the first time in quite a while, I remembered how it felt to be a wife instead of just a friend. For both of us, holding and being held took away any further need to fight and we lay on the bed finally listening to one another. We could not know at that moment, when all seemed finally right with our world, that in less than twenty-four hours a thoughtless mistake would have our whole family distraught and frantic.

On the following day my children and I ate lunch at the halfway point between home and Catherine's place in Guelph. Michael would return home, while I switched cars to go and stay over with Catherine. The previous night's sharing had left me feeling close to Carl and on such a blustery day I was especially eager to check in with Carl after supper and be sure he was okay.

But Carl was not home. Not at 6:30 and not at 8:30. Our phone lines had never been so busy. By 9:30, Michael was worried as well and began phoning around to track his Dad down. We all figured he had spent the day with Rick doing some kind of work for some kind of customer, but that was the sum of our conclusions. There had been a few tense discussions in the last few months about being reachable, and Carl had agreed to always have his cell phone with him or at least check it frequently in case anyone needed him. But by 10:30 with still no word, both Michael and I had talked to Rick's wife Marg who was also worrying. The weather up there was very bad she told us.

"They've gone to a sports bar or something," Stuart said, and Catherine and I insisted "No. You don't know Carl. He doesn't do that kind of thing. And he would never stay out of touch with his family. Something awful has happened." Visions of the little Tracker upside down in a ditch haunted us, and soon after eleven I asked Michael to check with the police. While he made calls, Catherine and I imagined increasingly bizarre scenarios including one where Carl might have gotten terrible news the previous day at his hospital checkup, and instead of telling us, had convinced Rick to help him commit suicide. Even through his depression a year earlier we had never imagined such a thing to be possible. I guess the more tired you are, the less logical you become.

The phone calls continued until a quarter to one, when Catherine and Stuart went to bed and Michael and I agreed that he would not call us unless there was news. I lay in bed sleepless. Carl would never stay out of touch that many hours in the daytime, let alone in a blizzard at night. Around two-thirty in the morning I finally got to sleep, and twenty minutes later the phone rang. It was Michael. His Dad had called and was on the way home from an out of town emergency. Whatever the emergency was, I thought, it couldn't be half as bad as the emergency he would be facing for breaking one of our cardinal family rules: 'You don't go anywhere, let alone out of town, without letting someone know where you are.' Amidst the fretting, I managed to get one more hour's sleep and then Catherine and I discussed what ought to happen communication-wise. Should we talk as a family? Should the kids give Carl and I some privacy to sort it out?

I was furious. "What I'd like to do," I told Catherine, "Is wait until he gets out of the car, and then jump in and drive away." Being in Guelph without a vehicle, I called him in the morning to come and get me, and his explanation about blizzards and telephones that didn't work did little to pacify me. He had gone out of town without letting anyone know where he was and causing all this worry. Furious had been downgraded, but I remained indignant.

The kids left about the time we expected Carl to arrive. They stayed away two hours. They wanted to know the battle was over before they came back. And it was. Once he was there in person we were able to talk through what happened and who was hurt and how to keep such a thing from ever happening again. If there was an up-side, it was that having this discussion in our daughter's home instead of in the privacy of our own bedroom opened our eyes. We had to recognize as a couple, how hard it was on our children, to see the struggles in our relationship. We talked on the way home. We talked more when we reached home.

My friend Ruth once told me she believes that little children need to see their parents together. "That's one of the reasons they will wander into the parents' bedroom in the middle of the night. They are looking to find their parents side by side."

Maybe big kids, even young adults, need the same reassurance. Michael had lived at home, away from home and at home again. Living with us, he could see that Carl and I were spending far more time together. Perhaps he noticed a change in each of us as individuals. He had a ringside seat for the private drama unfolding in our marriage. But Catherine and Stuart lived at a distance. Having shared my worry the night Carl 'disappeared' and having not seen us since the unpleasant discussion the following morning, they found it hard to trust that we were returning to who we used to be. Parents should not expose small children to their private battles. Had we made a dreadful mistake in airing our dirty laundry in front of our adult children? Maybe, but did we have a choice, given the circumstances? Carl and I tasted the generous portions of regret heaped on our plates.

We had moved forward in the last couple of weeks. We were on our way to being *side by side* again. We were thinking as a couple, and slowly figuring out what was required to get our relationship back on track. There had always been a part of me which found it hard to ask for help or support. Asking for what I needed, even from my own husband, felt awkward and uncomfortable. Carl was starting to find his way back to me. But months of feeling unheard when I explained how out of touch I felt, had left me unable to trust. We had several heart to heart talks and both did some soul searching.

I thought long and hard about the kind of communications Carl and I were having. In future I would ask myself, and suggest to Carl that he should also ask me, two questions, whenever I became upset: *What are you feeling? What do you need?*

Over the next three days, these two questions diffused two or three situations which could have turned into fights. The answer to the first question was almost always 'sad' or 'insecure'. The answer to the second came from a part of me I hardly recognized, a part which felt like a child. "This must be the inner child you hear so much about," I thought.

In the wee hours of Easter morning I wrote in my journal:

> The inner child, who is now out, is more easily brought to emotion than the person I always thought myself to be. I weep easily and often, and seek comfort from Carl, and this is bringing some healing into our marriage. It's as if my mind was engaged before, but without being in contact with my heart.
> What am I feeling right now? Appropriately for Easter Day, I feel hopeful. What do I need? I need to use my time with Carl for holding hands and going forward.

Trust Fund

*The bank account of trust we built between us in small deposits over the
years, began to shrink. In your dark place you were in no position to
invest, or save, or build up credit,
or even heed my frantic notices: "Sir: Your funds are running low."
And then, before the reserves ran out,
You suddenly extended such securities
Bonds of love, collateral of reassuring words
Guaranteed to earn interest, pledging strength and protection.
And no vaults could be found, large enough to hold such great fortune.*

I began to gain some balance by looking at my wants in a new way ... as needs. It was hard to do this as I had to guard against a toxic anxiety which whispered in my head, "This might be selfish. Why should you get to put yourself first?"

"No," the healthier part of me confronted the anxious voice. "If I would want it for a treasured child, then it is okay to want it for myself."

On the first day of April we woke to a startling return of winter wonderland. This was a day when I loved having my computer by the window to see the Christmas card scene outside.

> I wrote to Helen:
> Carl is trying hard to reconnect so we can rebuild our marriage. My sense of self-worth has been terribly damaged in the last while, and I am picking up the pieces now, but we both see that I am a different person in these last two weeks. Not sure who will emerge from the cocoon but it had better be a butterfly and she'd better be strong.

Solace

The sudden change of season was a marvel to everyone. On the radio they said: "We interrupt this spring to bring you ... summer." In a two week period we had experienced both a heavy snowfall and temperatures approaching thirty degrees. At the North Acre and at Moo Alley, we had always watched a particular shrub for the first leaves of spring. This year by mid-April, the signal branch was bursting into leaf. On the neighbouring country roads frogs sang their hearts out, and there was a constant cooing of doves outside the kitchen window.

The world outside had been released from winter, but for an entire month I had fought a losing battle with pain. Low backache was a chronic condition for me but I could not think of any physical cause for this unfamiliar pain higher in the back. I looked up information on spiritual connections to the upper back: forgiveness and compassion were stressed. I was preoccupied with pain, but as far as I was able, I tried to think about my connection to others and see my relationships as places for healing.

> Journal Entry April 16/02:
> Let me see judgment and anxiety as misplaced energy, and recognize the threat they pose to the body. Let me release unfinished business, and open mind, body, and spirit to God's energy.

We drove over country roads to see friends a few miles away. It was the loveliest of evenings, but in the car the persistent aching dominated my every thought. "Just let me get where we're going," I begged. Maybe getting out of the car would help. But once in the house, I couldn't stand having to be on my feet. "If only I could sit down." Sitting at last, the pain was too much to cope with. "I need the visit to be over so I can go home."

None of this was said out loud, but my body language must have been eloquent. When we got home Carl vowed he would take a *kill-or-cure* approach. He was able to reduce the intensity of a headache by finding a knot beneath the skin and pressing on it.

I lay face down across the bed while he ran his hands over my back. "There's a long ridge beneath the skin," he exclaimed. "Is that the sore place?" Carl pressed hard on the ridge, massaging it vigorously. The aching did not disappear but subsided enough to allow the first real relief in two weeks. I felt so much better that I could not sleep, and roamed the house for hours. I wrote Carl a thank you note, then a poem. To be free from pain should not to be taken for granted. It is a great blessing.

Solace

Unwilling to sit quiet by the bedside
Pain crept beneath the covers,
Spent every night whining at me
to wake up and pay attention.
Mornings it followed me from bed
dogging my every step
pressing closer through the day
demanding acknowledgement
insisting on recognition.

Greedily it ate my time
growing larger through the hours
pushing aside my consciousness
until by evening
Icouldhardlyseparateitfrommeanymore.

And then with warning hands you grabbed it by the neck
shook it hard and cut it down to size,
escorted it to a more seemly distance
cautioned it to keep its place.
freed me from the crushing presence
gave me room to breathe again.

Journal entry April 23/02:

> I have been thinking a lot about strength. The weakness in my back remains a concern although the area which aches has reduced from what it was a week ago. I keep wondering about the connection between bearing a burden emotionally, and having my back hurting and going into spasm. A friend reminded me recently that I did not need to stay strong for others. But others can only watch a certain amount of distress before they back away from it, so I save the larger part of my emotional pain for when I am alone or when I am with Carl. I think he does this as well. You have to have a pretty strong connection to someone to let them look into the depths of your hurt and sadness.

When Carl tells me he is dying, and other family members tell me they don't think that is true, and doctors tell me nothing, I feel as if I'm being torn in three pieces. Whatever is the case, this is a time in my life when I want more than ever before to spend time with my husband. Both of us try to concentrate as much as we can on living in the here and now.

Even so, there are occasions when my mind escapes into the future, dragging my heart along behind it. The emotional separation of the last year and our struggle to find one another again have been draining. But struggle brings its own reward. We love one another more than ever before in our whole lives. We are more up front with each other now than ever before. And we have both changed a great deal as individuals.

I once saw myself as a steady, reflective person who could be counted on to remain calm, think things through and talk things out. But since the 'escape of the inner child' I hardly know what my next response might be. Feelings are right at the surface and they come from some deep place I've known was there but seldom looked into.

Carl, on the other hand, has always shown strong feelings. He tended to react suddenly. And now, he thinks things through more than he used to, and explains his thoughts to me in quiet times together. "Have we exchanged roles?" we ask each other.

One Sunday morning early, Carl announced plans for that afternoon when he would be going with Rick out to the farm where they sometimes worked. Disappointment flooded through me. He had worked all week. This morning I had to play for the Sunday service. I had counted on having time with Carl in the afternoon.

Sitting side by side on the edge of the bed we tried to unearth reasons for the sorrow I was feeling. "This is a time which should be ours." Instead Carl was spending this time in other places, with other people. Together we figured out that Sundays after church had special meaning for me. Sundays were the day when in our earlier life we would have a special time for one another and do things with our family. The day when my friends were with families and husbands.

Of course I knew single women. I respected their independence. I admired the way each one had walked through her own particular pain. I valued their friendship but in them was reflected an image I feared ... an image of a future I had not chosen. I saw that many of them had not chosen a life alone either. They had chosen partners and those partners were gone. Although it was out of proportion to what was happening right in that moment, I dreaded coming home without Carl being with me or waiting for me. Coming home alone, I saw before me a long future with Carl missing from it, and it was this truth I could hardly bear to look at. My heart crumpled but work called.

There was nothing to do but shove the broken pieces down somewhere out of sight and try to pull together an outward shell in order to do my work and face people. But Carl and I both knew that all those little bits remained inside, held together only enough to keep things looking normal to the world.

Through the little sorrows and big losses, we were beginning to learn that we were strong enough to bear burdens, even ones which seemed insupportable. We were learning to trust our hearts to see clearly what we needed to see, and accept what for now remained hidden. But at the same time, did we need to understand that the journey was less about strength, and more about balancing? After all, no amount of strength would keep a tight-rope walker on the wire if he could not hold his balance. We had to keep putting one foot ahead of the other. I knew that day and I needed to remember in future, that the broken pieces were still down there. But if I looked down I might lose my balance. Right now, I could not risk it. Eyes ahead. One foot in front of the other.

Part 2

Getting Back on Track

Bad Memories, Good Dreams

Although it is taken for granted by many on the Bruce Peninsula that hunting is 'what men do', Carl could never have been a hunter. Often over the years wild animals appeared to sense that quality in him, approaching him without fear. I have heard the gentle way he speaks to creatures, wild and tame alike. He grew up in a culture where the groundhog in the back yard would have been shot, but he would be more likely to feed it than harm it. For years Carl had carried a shovel in the car. When he saw a dead animal by the road he would remove it from public view. "It was a life. It deserves some respect," he said.

Over the course of our marriage, Carl occasionally referred to bad childhood memories associated with his farm upbringing. A vague discomfort made him wonder if there could be more than he was recalling but he was never sure. One day in early May, seeing a dead cow by the roadside touched some innermost painful memory. He could not get the creature out of his mind and that night described what he had seen, his degree of distress out of proportion with the sight of a dead cow.

I sat beside him on the bed. From somewhere a question came to me seemingly unrelated to what he was saying, but I asked it anyway: "Has anyone ever made you do something you did not want to do?"

A response rose from the deepest core of his being. I stayed quiet, watching him struggle, finally able to tell me only that the question had dredged up long buried memories of being made to watch the slaughtering of farm animals. There was nothing I could do but stay close and accept that this was a pain he needed to exorcise on his own. When he was ready, I decided, he would tell me, even though I wasn't sure I wanted to hear.

It took until the next night for him to gather the strength to be able to talk about the terror his child-self had felt. Vivid scenes came back to him. Sounds of pain echoed through his mind. Even breathing became difficult as he relived the panic of a child who loved animals, forced to watch their suffering. The fact that many farm children, particularly boys, had to see similar scenes, did not make the damage any less. He could not turn off the sights and sounds, he told me.

He described how the men had taken a cavalier attitude to the slaughter, making grotesque jokes, perhaps because they did not know any other way to deal with what had to be done. I asked if he could mentally dissolve the pictures. It was more like a "video in his head," he said. "Then if you can't shut it down," I suggested, "add to the video. Consciously put in a sequel where you grow up and treat animals with respect and dignity. Because that is what really happened."

Carl apologized for falling apart the previous night. But it took more courage to 'fall apart' than it would have taken to keep shoving the memories down.

I am thankful I have no video-tape of suffering animals playing in my head. But there is a 'tape' there all the same, one which insists that without Carl's time and attention I am not okay. That can't be healthy.

I suspect that most of us have a voice we play in our unconscious mind. Somewhere in my brain the message repeats far too often: "A bad thing happened. Is it going to happen over and over?" I need to add to my own tape: "No, because you are not going to allow it to happen again. But if it does happen, you are going to be given the strength and resources to deal with it."

There is a poem I love on that subject:

When we come to the edge of all the light we know,
And must take a step into the darkness of the unknown,
One of two things we must be sure of:
Either we will find something to stand firm on
Or we will be taught to fly.

Dr. Patrick Overton

Thankfully though, our minds are able to go in many directions. I have been a daydreamer since I was a child. Over the years daydreaming receded to some deep corner of my consciousness. Still, one day I found myself in the bathtub picturing God out there (in there?) Smiling. I didn't mean for that s to have a capital, and it could have been a simple error in typing. Or maybe when God smiles He/She/It insists on a capital. Anyway, the reason God is smiling is because of the fantasy I was just having.

Probably, the bathtub is one of the world's better places to dream. I have always felt free to take baths at any hour of the day. Often, if I was up early with Carl and he left for the day, even if the sky was still dark, it just might be a good time for a bath. Or maybe I looked at the clothes I had on and noticed they could go in with the laundry I just threw in the machine. Might as well take a bath. And of course, evening is a wonderful time to immerse yourself in warm fragrant bathwater, unless you just took a bath in order to wash your hair at three o'clock in the afternoon.

There in the Not-so-Deep Woods, bathing was more active than passive. Baths at our house took a bit of effort as the water pressure was a little weak and so we had to forget those movie scenes where the heroine is neck-deep in bubbles. In our bathtub, if you wanted to stay wet, you had to keep running the tap to warm up the water and splashing water over your body with a scooping motion. Wait, maybe a bucket would be a good idea. But there goes my mind again, fantasizing.

So there I was, imagining God smiling at my fantasy (it's a fantasy within a fantasy, you see?) that my book has been published. Not only that. It is being read all over Grey County and even beyond.

God encourages me: "Go on. Dream. It's okay to see yourself successful."

"But God," I argue, "am I not being vain? Or ambitious? I mean there must be a sin in there somewhere."

"Who do you think put you on this path in the first place?" God answers. "Who do you think set you down in a family of book lovers, and showed you that Sunday school paper which paid real money for your little child poems, and even had Liberty magazine publish your essay in grade twelve?"

"Wasn't that just to make a point with that arrogant English teacher who gave it a zero?" I ask.

"Sometimes, I like to do more than one thing at once," says God, "I think they call it multi-tasking." Then God disappears. Probably some other woman in a bathtub needs permission for a fantasy of her own.

I am left to wonder if God knows about the whole bag of Easter eggs on the table in my writing corner. "Oh for heaven's sake!" a Voice interjects (God is really into this multi-tasking thing). "A small indulgence now and then is allowed too. You really have to learn to dream, kid."

Exploring a Marriage

Deep in a bottom drawer I found a pair of notebooks we kept twelve years earlier in a marriage encounter weekend. Convinced that we had changed within our relationship in just a few months, I was amazed at the degree to which we were, nevertheless, the same people with the same concerns as we had been a dozen years ago. Even then, the notebook told me, I had been watchful concerning negative patterns. The issues might have been different but the fears were the same. If a negative pattern were allowed to persist, what did that mean for the future?

In the notebook I read about the Carl I knew ten years ago, creative, intelligent and funny. I had described myself: growing in confidence but still reluctant to take risks, playing the role of organizer in our family, thinking I had to hold it all together.

"Focus on the feeling," said the notebook. "Never argue with a feeling." Well of course, I know that now, I decided, as I read through the book. But I wondered to what degree I understood this idea at the time I was writing it down.

The notebook talked about our closeness, and our need to be individuals without letting that come at a cost of being with each other. It cautioned about letting daily distractions interfere with our time as a couple and asked if we were sometimes putting ourselves last?

That marriage encounter weekend has never held fond memories for us as a couple. All autonomy was removed as others decided on our behalf when we would eat, sleep, or communicate. We were shut in a hotel room, meeting with a group of other couples when told to, and not allowed to leave our room or to know when anything was to happen. However, being confident people, we left the room when we felt shut in and took strolls in the parking lot ... not far, but enough to get a bit of fresh air when we needed it.

The couples running the workshop shared their feelings with the large group, modeling a way of communicating with one another. Participants were asked questions about our thoughts and feelings which we were to answer in writing, and then share with our partners in the privacy of our room. The exploration of ourselves and our relationship should have been a positive experience, but for Carl, whose self-image was low, it dragged up issues he was not ready to face. His degree of agitation was one I had never seen in him before. I would see it again several years in the future when he would be ready to face the painful memories from his childhood. For now, his anguish was bewildering to me and he needed more help than I could give.

We called the room of the couple who had been assigned to work with us if needed. They came down to our room but did not seem to understand Carl's distress. At the dinner table, I turned to the Anglican priest who was in charge. "My husband is in difficulty," I told him. "We need some psychological support." I might as well have said: "We need more potatoes." He answered politely but it did not seem to have registered that there was an actual problem.

We finished lunch and attended the group session long enough to see that these people were following a script which would work in most cases but not for us. It was clear that there would be no support. We looked at one another and without a word, rose from our chairs and left the session. From our room we called our minister and went straight to his house, describing the weekend we had just been through. "Most people," he explained to us, "are not as intense as you two. You throw yourselves one hundred percent into whatever you are asked to do. If you combine this request to explore your feelings with the removal of your rights to make decisions for yourselves, and add to it painful memories from the past, you end up feeling troubled and anxious."

We left his house feeling calmer and looking forward to an afternoon where we could be free of that hotel room and the artificial controls which had gone with it. When I talked months later to a couple who had been at a different marriage encounter weekend, they were puzzled. They had not been sleep deprived or told when they could or could not eat or leave the room. The negatives had not existed for them. They had only been given the excellent questions to ask one another and explore at whatever level they were ready for.

Still, as I looked back at the ten-year old notebook I knew that there was much of value in it. It painted a picture of my love for this man at a time when we had been married for twenty years, a time when we were both in good health and had both children living at home. In the notebook I found a letter answering the question: *Why I want to go on living?* And: *Why I want to go on living with you?* I left a note for my husband.

> *Dear Carl,*
>
> *There is so much to live for and you are at the top of the list, the letter began. I can never wait to get to you with my news, good or bad. You are my support. You make me feel safe and protected. There is no one else who is special enough, loved enough, for me to let down my guard the way I do with you. There are others I trust, but not like you.*
>
> *I respect you ... your wit, intelligence, humour, your drive to work hard, compassion for little kids and animals, reliability and sensitivity. You are my balance (just as I, I believe, am yours) my security, my valued partner, in our marriage, as a teacher, and at choir practice ... two out of my three jobs. I love you. People get tired of hearing me talk about you all the time, I'm sure, but you fill so much of my heart and mind.*

Carl's letter to me spoke of not being able to picture a life without me:

> "You are the stabilizer for my off the wall and I am the devil's advocate for some of your ideas," he wrote. "I started off looking for a friend, and ended up with a consultant, then lover, wife, workmate and organizer, but mostly best friend. I guess I need to be reminded that you are the most special person in the world to me. You are a person who chose to spend your life with me. It's my responsibility to make sure that your life with me is good enough for you to participate fully. I can listen and perhaps clarify and support you. I know that I am difficult when I'm up, and I'm positive I'm impossible when I'm down. I know you do your best to be loving and supportive in both these situations."

Reading Carl's notebook, reminded me of the long way he had come in the last dozen years. I married a man who truly did have a lot of ups and downs. His personality was in all likelihood borderline bipolar. We had talked about this many times. But as I looked back on our life together I knew that I would never have traded the joy of Carl's ups in order to escape the downs. Over the years Carl had brought laughter with him to most places he went. His colleagues, his friends, and mostly his wife, were willing to see the shadow side on occasion in order to enjoy the more frequent brightness.

And now, having experienced together the shadow side of both health and marriage, we had perhaps come to appreciate more, those years before these twin trains got so out of control. Just as with Carl's brighter and darker sides, it was only in having seen the shadow that we grew to recognize the light. We understood better now, what good health meant to our lives. We had come to cherish our marriage, far too precious to take for granted. If the health train was still out of our control, we could at least breathe a sigh of relief over the marriage train, no longer going downhill at all, but on the level, heading down the track with both of us, at least for the time being, at the controls, holding hands.

Wedding Bells

When we started planning Catherine and Stuart's wedding six months ago we had all wondered how long Carl would still be able to walk. In those six months he had lost his balance often, stumbled at times, and even fallen down a flight of outdoor stairs at a building center. He and Rick divided chores according to which ones could be done in a sitting position. But as slowly and unevenly as Carl now walked, he would be able to walk his daughter down the aisle to her new husband.

Tall windows encircled the reception hall looking over a large reflecting pool on one side. From the opposite windows the west lawn of the Arboretum stretched out, with lilacs finally in bloom after a cold spring. We could see the big tree where the bride and groom would stand tomorrow. The sun set and before long a choir of frogs outside the windows serenaded us while we worked.

My brother Jody tuned up his guitar and we tried out some music as Stuart's family, the Robertsons, put together an arbor, and our sister-in-law Evie concocted elaborate and graceful floral decorations for the head table. I had long ago removed the shoes from my sore feet, and hoped the Robertsons understood that their son was marrying into a family where comfort was a lot more important than elegance. Stuart's Mom, Friede, was trying to give away the considerable remains of a huge cake she had brought for the rehearsal picnic: "I have another one just as big at home," she told us.

The wedding day itself was a mix of hurrying and relaxing. Carl described putting together centerpieces in record time. "There we were," he explained, "slamming roses into vases." But there was quiet time later to wander around the grounds of the Bed and Breakfast where we were staying, taking photographs in the bright sunshine. During the more formal picture taking before the wedding, a train thundered by. Catherine had heard that it is good luck to see a train on your wedding day, and it reminded me of my father who was an engineer, so the train was a happy interruption.

Compared to our two old, constantly-breaking-down vehicles full of groceries or tools, the beautiful white car borrowed to drive the bridal party from place to place was sleek and polished. Perhaps that's why the photographer wanted photos with the car.

With the final photo taken, he left for the Arboretum. Renata, bridesmaid number two, looked down and gasped. Somehow, oil from the car had gotten onto the front of Catherine's wedding gown. Despite her young age, Renata, had certain Martha Stewart qualities. With products borrowed from the owner of the B&B, she sponged at Catherine's dress until the worst stains were removed. Crisis number one, over. We had lost ten minutes but hurried now to climb into cars for the fifteen minute drive to the Arboretum.

Crisis number two was still to come. Jody looked worried: "I can't find the music anywhere," he told us, "and the keyboard doesn't seem to be in the same key as the guitar." We were so concerned about the disappearing music I lost track of Jody's second concern. Quickly, Evie scribbled down the words of the song (how wonderful that she knew them!) and I double checked on the piano indoors that I would be able to play the piece by ear. The photographer suggested that Stuart's brother Kevin escort me to my seat. Friede was not seated at all as she was absorbed in taking videos.

The cello began playing the soothing melody of the Pachelbel Canon. We turned to see Catherine on her father's arm. My mother said later that just as they started their walk across the lawn, the wind caught Catherine's dress and she appeared to be floating down the aisle.

Carl slid in beside me and in a moment it was time for him to sing. Jody played the opening bars and I joined in on the keyboard. He and I exchanged hurried, and worried, glances. The two instruments were in different keys. What could we do? I kept going. Jody stopped. Carl sang. It was lovely anyway. But we missed hearing Jody's music. People must have thought it was unusual to have a guitar there to play a two bar intro.

Through the ceremony, Stuart kept one eye on minister Keith and the other on the arbour over their heads. A light weight twelve foot structure might easily have sailed away on such a breezy day, but it held in place, and they said their vows, Catherine weeping through the words which held such meaning for her. As Keith pronounced them husband and wife, the sun which had gone in during the ceremony, suddenly burst out.

Never was there a more disorganized receiving line. But that is characteristic of our family who cannot even pass dishes all in the same direction at a holiday dinner table. Carl could not be found for a little as he was visiting with everyone he encountered along the way. Was Friede in the line or was she still taking pictures? I don't even remember. But greeting each dear face was important, knowing they were all there to share our special celebration, even neighbours Lee and Ruth who were shuttling between our location and another wedding an hour away. I had visions of Lee driving like a madman and turning to Ruth: "How many more weddings do we have to get to today?"

There were aunts and uncles we don't often get to see, and young friends from the kids' university days to meet for the first time. The navy satin gown was the most beautiful dress I had ever worn in my life, but even then it was too great a challenge for me to appear elegant. My stockings, advertised on the package as *stay-ups* were more like *fall-downs* and I had removed them and shoved them into my tiny bag. This meant that the far too tight straps on my new sandals were now cutting into my feet, gouging angry red crisscross patterns into the flesh. I would endure them for two more hours before removing them to go barefoot once again. After all, the mother of the bride cannot go to a buffet table in bare feet, no matter how exquisite her dress is.

As hard as it was to gather sixty-some people together for a photo, we managed it. The photographer moved people hither and yon, bantering with the crowd to get them into place on a hillside in front of the building. A bit later one of the grandmas was heard to say: "I'll stand anywhere except on that hill." Standing at a tilt in fancy shoes is a challenge at any age.

All that remained was to enjoy the tasty dinner, listen to the swing band music the kids had chosen, and marvel at the beautiful surroundings. Each round table had a bouquet of pink and cream roses on its white linen tablecloth. There were candles and flowers everywhere, and outside a half moon reflected in the pond. The frogs were joyfully singing again, and why not?

On Retreat

With the honeymooners off to the east coast for a week, I headed down to their Guelph apartment to look after pets. Everywhere little posters offered instruction. By the fish bowl a fish cartoon announced: "I like to eat. Please give me seven pellets each day you are here." A drawing of a cat by the door warned me never to open it without looking down in case the 'Wild Rose' was trying to escape.

Rose, though fully grown, had a tiny frame with no fat at all, only long ginger and white fur clinging to a bony little body. Small protruding ridges above her eyes gave her a miniature Neanderthal look. She had a nervous nature and energy to spare so that the kids were always worried about her darting out an open door. But Rose was far too busy to make an escape plan. She was engrossed in perfecting her high jump techniques, launching herself at the birdcage and clinging to the side. The two little birds sat silent at the back of the cage, shivering I expect. A squirt bottle was on hand to discourage the jump-and-leer game, but Rose had the safe distance measured to the millimeter. She knew exactly how far that spray bottle would reach and how long it would take me from any point in the apartment to get within striking distance.

Not all my time was needed for the care and feeding of three cats, two birds, and a fish. I had plenty of quiet alone time, a good chance to do some serious reflecting. I thought about who I was, how I came to be this person, and where I wanted to go next. I thought back to the time my father was dying. I remembered people from my early teaching years and how they included me in their life. I thought about the earliest years of our marriage and the effect being a mother had on me.

Words people had spoken to me and about me came back to me now, and as the same themes surfaced again and again, I felt that I should set some goals based on what I had learned: a) grow in confidence; b) deepen connections with other like-minded people; and c) choose my words carefully being mindful of their effect on people.

I looked over the goals. The first one seemed kind of vague. Did I have any idea how I was going to accomplish this? Number two should be a joy. Maybe they would all be a joy. Maybe all goals should be a joy. Even as I wrote the third goal down, I recognized that my shoot-from-the-hip style of communicating might need to change. Although I was not impulsive in my actions, I tended to speak without thinking things through, and this goal would test my good intentions. It would be hard work.

Two days I thought about these things, finally writing to Carl to share my conclusions:

> Dear Carl:
>
> Being by myself for this length of time has felt like a *retreat* offering a chance to think about choices and changes. I think I have to work at seeing myself not just as half of a couple, but as an individual with separate needs and resources.
>
> You mentioned recently that I have lost confidence, and I know this is true, Still, I have no doubt that you, of all the people in my life, offer me a sustaining love. I know that you are sorting through your own life issues right now, and that this is not an easy time for you. Let me hold you safe. Let's remind one another that when we have those dark moments, they will pass.
>
> Thank you for being my husband and my friend.

Performance

So did you ever think you'd get to play the prince
so late in your career?
Waken the sleeper with a kiss
Murmur encouragements in her ear.
Open her eyes to a new and different world
Teach her, through love, to look beneath and past
the lumps and bumps incurred by body and soul,
and see herself as beautiful at last,
longed for and longing, the seeker and the prize,
not understanding how she changed so fast.

And do you understand the import of the role?
And why you could not take it on before?
And who will be affected by the way you played the part?
And how you came to touch the sleeper's soul?

Issues

"Brain or knee?" people asked whenever we spoke of an upcoming medical appointment. There were times now when Carl could not find the words he needed but surely this was unrelated to the brain condition, which doctors agreed should only affect "anything below the neck." Walking had become so much more difficult for Carl. His muscles and ligaments sustained repeated injuries from unexpected lurches sideways when messages about balance did not get from brain to leg, and pain was a constant companion.

Carl went often to see the physiotherapist. He would come home from these sessions mindful of pain and sorrowful in mood. I had to be careful never to grumble about household chores as this only made him more aware of what he could no longer do. Already, each physiotherapy appointment pointed out the decline in abilities looming so large in Carl's mind. "Sometimes," he told me, "if I'm away from home, I phone you just in order to 'dial up my security'." I didn't feel strong enough to be anyone's security. I was not the calm steady person I used to be.

My emotions were close to the surface in a way I was still not used to and Carl's nerves frayed with pain. Both of us felt psychologically fragile and it took very little to make either of us feel threatened. Keeping our marriage connected still took a conscious effort. We kept asking ourselves and each other: "What are you feeling?" "What do you need?" To simply say: "I feel threatened. I need you to hold me," sounds easy enough, but it takes practice to be this direct with one another. For me, feeling vulnerable even made it hard to maintain eye contact.

"Look at me," Carl insisted, reaching to tilt my chin up so that I could not look at my feet. "How do you think it feels to talk to someone who won't look at you?" Keeping my head down was a way of drawing inside myself. "We're bouncing sadness and anxiety back and forth like a rubber ball," I told him. There were patterns within patterns, and they needed to be interrupted but my lack of strength and resourcefulness left me feeling troubled. And yet, why should it be shameful to need support? We might need more than a single lifeline at a time when we were drifting in such rough waters. I thought of us as castaways in a storm. I wanted someone to rescue us.

> Journal entry June 18/02:
> We try to use our connection to each other to heal and grow, but it's as if we are stranded on an island. I think we need a wider connection to friends we can talk with meaningfully. And I think spending time outdoors by lake, forest, and meadow, might also help.

Perhaps my emotional turmoil was like a labouring towards the birth of a stronger, more trusting, clearer thinking individual. Breathing techniques help in a birth process. Maybe if I could use calm slow regular breathing to compose myself it would help. I remembered from childbirth classes all those years ago how concentrating so much on the breathing was supposed to let us detach from the pain of contractions. Could I learn to focus completely on the feelings and stop giving energy to where they came from?

Just two years ago, having a spiritual goal was a foreign concept for me. Now, I was doing a check on *who I was* and *where I was*, every few weeks. I explored several areas of my life using the headings Spiritual, Marriage, Family and Friends, Writing, and House. The needs in the house category, looked more like a To Do list, but writing them down made me feel less likely to lose track.

In all, I had listed twenty-five directions to go in. "Let's just see how many of them I have been making progress in," I decided a few days later. The final tally was a surprise:

Spiritual 2
Marriage 4
Family and Friends 3

Home 4
Writing 2

Fifteen out of twenty-five. Not bad at all. Without this reality check I would have guessed that I had given very little to the Home needs, an area I found discouraging and one where I often gave my time reluctantly. But look how hard I had been trying. And did I just cancel out a negative thought with some positive affirmations? I really *was* doing better.

All that summer I asked myself: "What's really going on here?" whenever I noticed expectations and judgments sneaking in to cloud my thinking. "It's feeling threatened that causes the distress," I explained to Carl. I wished one of us could just say to the other: "I feel threatened," and the other one would respond: "What do you need me to do?"

Issues

Abandonment and Trust
creep hand in hand around the edges of our consciousness.
Strange companions
bound together by the willful murmurings of our souls.
One crying: "Stay with me, stay with me."
The other rebelling: "If you believe in me, let me go."
Unworthy accomplices sneaking through the alleys of our minds
silently taunting by their very presence.

But now we see them for what they are,
And we challenge their very presence,
their oh so very unwanted presence
and not for much longer will we allow these twisted twins
to slither down the pathways of suppressed self.
Shine the light on them. If there's anything they hate, it's Light.

Journal entry August 4/02:

Exposing feelings of being unsafe, to the light of *how it ought to be* is a painful process. How to keep from dragging in judgments, expectations, feelings of unworthiness? I have to get a better balance between my own need to feel safe and my ability to give Carl the space he needs. When we do not get a reasonable amount of time together, it only takes a few days before I *disconnect* emotionally and then the next instance where I feel let down becomes a trigger for hurt and disappointment. Our pattern is that Carl talks me through that hurt, and then usually within a day or two, experiences a crisis of his own. Patterns can be dangerous. Is this one bringing about healing, or just causing a cycle of emotional pain for both of us?

Michael told me once about a Tai Chi teaching regarding conflict. Stages are represented by colours:

> white - give it space (back off for a while)
> yellow – add warmth (will kindness help?)
> red - state your position (know that this may lead to more conflict)
> black - the relationship is in danger of ending

Many times in the past two years Carl and I had been in the red stage. For a little while we had even been in the black. The black was a stage I did not want to return to. But how could anyone get closer without stating their position and hearing their partner's? Or was I confusing the need to understand a person's thinking with the need to understand his feelings? Did I need to make my position known? Or only my hurt and sadness?

I wondered whether the colour stages might also apply to friendships: Do friendships have to go through a shadow side, perhaps in a miniature version of what intimate relationships do? I thought a lot about the marriages of people I knew. While I had no magic window into any of them, it looked to me as if many marriages were more steady than ours but in that steadiness sacrificed the joys. Can we really have one end of the spectrum without the other?

For my birthday eighteen women crowded onto our deck on a beautiful Sunday afternoon, talking and laughing, and delighting in one another's company. All of them knew about Carl's health situation. A few of them knew of the struggles in our marriage. Several people had brought poems and sayings to share with the group.

Our good friend Bonnie gave out cards which spoke of our walk through life, and how, even when we fall down we need to get back up and keep dancing. I'm sure this was an instruction to the spirit rather than the body, but a few nights later, Carl and I found ourselves in our dining room playing a scratchy old LP record of a longtime favourite tune: *At Last*. With Carl's legs likely to stumble, we could only *dance* with feet in a fixed position. But we held one another and felt the sweetness in the music:

> *My love, let's make this moment last,*
> *No future and no past.*
> *Just us, just now, my love.*

The previous night, Carl had suggested playing charades. The idea of a husband and wife spending their evening playing charades seemed so outlandish, so delightful, so typically Carl. I shook my head, laughing, but Carl started the game anyway. The harder I laughed, the more insistent Carl became, holding up fingers in front of my face: "Four words ... first word ..."

Michael told me the next day he had started down the hallway, approaching our room carefully, unsure whether he was hearing laughter or hysterical crying. I guess we sounded like a small but wild house party. Insistently Carl held his hand up: "Four words ... first word ..."

And so we faced the unknown future, recognizing that there are days we cry, but some days we laugh, and we hold one another, and we dance.

Life is Only...

Carl tossed his wallet and keys onto the shelf in the front closet and bent to remove his boots. He looked discouraged. "I tipped the riding mower over on my leg." I looked quickly to see which leg and noted it was the bad one ... no sense messing up both legs at the same time.

The bruising eventually gave way to a sore which would not heal and Carl seemed to be at the hospital every day or two ... though not always the same hospital. He had appointments for his brain condition, appointments for his knee, and now urgent trips to Wiarton and Owen Sound, whichever direction the day's errands demanded, for the wound on his leg. He was seeing four or five different doctors, some locally and some in Toronto, and the various doctors ordered various tests.

One day Carl received word that he needed to go to Owen Sound for a scan. Sitting on the examining table he removed shoe and sock on the injured leg and waited for the technician to arrive. "What on earth are you doing?" the man asked, and Carl explained that he was just getting ready for the x-ray. "On your neck?" asked the dumbfounded technician.

The hole in Carl's leg was perfectly round, and, they told us, very deep. A third round of intravenous antibiotics was needed. Legs were causing trouble on every front. Carl was shuttling between hospitals to have the ulcer on his shin tended. My mother, with no doctor of her own, was going to the clinic downtown each day for needles for phlebitis. And when I dropped in to see our friend Dianne Barry one afternoon I found her on the couch with a broken bone in her foot.

All these people needing support! I thought of the poem Katie, Carl's mother, used to tell us. We asked her where it came from and our only answer was that she had "known this poem forever".

Life is only froth and bubble
Two things stand like stone:
Kindness in another's trouble,
Courage in your own.

Adam Lindsay Gordon

I wanted to show *kindness in another's trouble* but my head was spinning from not knowing who to go to first. The courage Katie's poem advised for our own trouble was also in short supply that autumn. Mostly I pretended that Carl was well (head-wise anyway). He had been in pain for so long with shredded ligaments in his knee. Finally a doctor said he could operate … next June. Next June? How would he manage this misery until next June when getting to next week sometimes seemed impossible. I had to keep repeating the words. They made me so angry. Next June.

Looking in my journal for words of reassurance, I found 'There is nothing left to fear.' But I was afraid. I didn't know if Carl would be strong enough to cope with this pain for such a long time. I didn't know if I could have compassion for his suffering without being dragged down by it. 'There is nothing left to fear,' said my journal, with a little note that as I wrote those words down so long ago I had looked at the clock and noticed that it was 6:34. I looked at the clock again. It was 7:34. The old sign. Someone was watching over us.

My childhood was spent in a house with the street number 1134. Whenever our life is about to become overly stressful, the 34's show up on clocks, highway mileage signs, bills in restaurants … just about anywhere there are numbers. I think of it as a message saying: "It will be okay in the end. Hang on." Can I get into that space where I really believe there is nothing left to fear? If we had been able to look ahead two or three years, we might have found quite a lot to fear. Sometimes it is just as well that we cannot see what lies ahead.

"I can't stand the pain," Carl told his physiotherapist. And full of good intentions, and *kindness in another's trouble* the man set out to locate a physician out of town. Staying with the local surgeon meant next June was the only option. The Toronto doctor did exploratory surgery. "I can't fix this," he admitted. "I'll send you on to another surgeon." If we had been able to predict the damage about to happen, we would have concluded there was plenty left to fear, only for the time being we didn't know it.

'C' Stands For ...

I wonder why so many of the qualities I admire begin with the letter C. There are lots of R's too, and more than a few L's, but the C's outnumber them all.

Being a communicator is one I value. Whether I am talking or writing, I try hard to get my point across. My kindergarten teacher once told my mother that if I thought I was right I would argue anyone into the ground. But being right is sometimes not worth the price you have to pay. I'd rather be understood than be 'right'. The words "I understand," if offered with sincerity, are powerful and husbands might be advised to keep this in mind during arguments with their wives.

When I think about qualities I appreciate most, I want to be clear in my thinking, confident in who I am, caring in my approach to others, and connected in increasingly deep ways to family and friends. So if I am working my way through the alphabet of qualities I am stuck on the letter c for sure. I also notice that these attributes I want to develop seem to be interconnected. For example, if I were truly clear in my thinking that would make me able to look with compassion at my self and others. If I were more confident would I not present myself in such a way that others would be inclined to deepen their connection with me?

> Journal entry Nov.28/02:
> My feelings lately are close to the surface and I identify more than I used to what is really going on. Carl and I communicate more honestly, though sometimes with less sensitivity than is needed. The connection between us is deeper than a year ago. The connection with friends is deeper too.

I could not look at Carl's health struggle without feeling compassion. But then all around us were people whose circumstances called out for compassion.

Maryann, a woman from Double Vision, our singing group, was fighting ovarian cancer. Tall and willowy, Maryann was a gentle person with a soft speaking voice and a lifelong delight in music. I remember once when there was some dissension between two of the women, seeing Maryann's eyes tear up. Some people wear their hearts on their sleeves, the saying goes. Maryann carried hers in her hands where its gentleness could be extended to whoever she was with. Maryann knew about compassion from the inside out.

The last time I had visited Maryann she was taking her chemo treatment in hospital. In the large room each recliner held a patient fighting his own personal battle. Seeing these ordinary people thrust into circumstances they never expected, helped me put in perspective my so much smaller complaints, my so much easier life.

Maryann lay back in her padded chair and I told her about a collection of music I had on computer: "Everything from Faure's Sicilienne to the Guess Who," I described and Maryann smiled at the thought. "While the music plays," I continued, "patterns in bright colours, much like a kaleidoscope, flash on and off the screen." Both of us hoped she could come out to the Lake to hear the music. "I'll put you in a rocking chair in front of the screen," I promised. But in the next few weeks she got too sick too fast and Maryann did not get to hear the songs as we had hoped.

I entered the funeral home looking for friends to sit with. I looked around for other singers from our group but didn't see any of them. A minute or two later, Donna, who had joined Double Vision just months before we disbanded, entered with husband Don. They sat down, one to my left and one to my right.

As people spoke their memories, tears slipped down my cheeks. I wished I could wipe them away but my arms were crossed at the wrists and Don was holding my right hand, Donna my left. The group of people in the chapel was surprisingly small. Don and Donna hardly knew Maryann, really, but they wanted to be here for me and for their friend Bert sitting on Donna's other side. It was fitting. Bert and I both had connections to Maryann through music, and Maryann would have loved Donna's beautiful singing.

Maryann's daughter offered a heartfelt tribute to her Mom, and Don squeezed my hand. I expect he was thinking of his own daughter just as I was thinking of mine. I know what it is to lose a parent at a young age. My Dad died when I was just fifteen.

When the service was over Don and Donna continued to stand on either side of me 'til the procession of funeral cars moved out. Then we went for a bowl of soup and a quiet chat. This was how they had chosen to spend their Saturday morning. These dear friends possessed all the C-qualities I might ever want to have, most of all, compassion.

Give Me Strength!

Carl's pain was just a fact of life so we were relieved when finally in a whirlwind of phone calls he got an appointment in Toronto to go over the MRI results on his knee and within days surgery was scheduled. Waiting until the following June, the alternative offered in Owen Sound, seemed unthinkable. What was truly unthinkable, and unknowable at the time, was that this decision would result in years of further suffering and near disastrous consequences.

Carl found the pain following the operation no worse than the pain prior to it, but was impatient to heal and walk better. We had a drop-in for friends soon after the surgery. As usual, all twenty of them wanted to sit in the same room at the same time. I have heard that Canadians will fill no more than seventy percent of a space ... but in our house, the sitting room usually sat vacant while everyone squeezed into the family room. The circle of rocking chairs pushed further and further back til it became twice as long as it was wide, no longer a circle, but an elongated oval big enough to hold everyone.

I hoped that seeing friends would help Carl to focus on something other than the slow healing of his knee. Thinking about being physically weak only reminded him that the future was very uncertain. His knee might heal, but what about the brain condition? He was experiencing periods of profound sadness such as we had both gone through a year before at the initial diagnosis.

"You don't understand what is happening to me," he insisted.

"I do, but I have a different focus. I used to value what you could do. Now I'm at a place in my life where I value more who you can be. And I see that you are the person on this earth who more than anyone else helps me to be who I can be."

"But who would want to be with me?" Carl asked.

He could not understand that being with him was what I had always wanted. It lay behind every fight we had. We never fought about in-laws, or money, or any of those other things so many couples battle about. Having time with my husband was the only thing in our relationship I saw as worth fighting for.

In the middle of the night I would find myself lying awake wishing I had chosen my words more wisely, wondering if it would have made a difference:

> *What I wish I'd said — These past few days circumstances have kept us apart too much. No one is to blame. But no one can 'fix it' either, except us. And to do that we need time together, not parallel time, but connecting time. For me that means holding and being held, talking and listening and sharing what I have been thinking or doing. The bottom line is that I miss you. I want to regain the closeness. I have read that "absence makes the heart grow fonder ... as long as it does not grow fond of the absence". This, I think, is your fear and maybe in a little way my own as well: that I might grow fond of the absence. Why would we ever let that happen when it is a simple matter of re-connecting through talk and touch?*

Did other people cycle through these destructive patterns? We would go along peacefully for a while, then lack of quality time together would trigger anxiety in me. My distress would cause Carl's self-blame issues to flare up, and we would throw these two balls of negative debris back and forth for a few days. We threw wildly, without nearly enough regard for one another's emotional safety. There would be two or three unpleasant discussions in a week's time until we would say to one another: "We cannot fight today. It's too much to bear. We need some peace."

Were we making any progress? Was there any other way to get past the stumbling blocks or was it necessary to go through that misery in order to find real peace? One thing we knew: the fights were about past hurts and future fears more than present issues. That couldn't be healthy. Surely we were mature enough to understand that *now is all we ever have*. Our hearts, bruised from before, frightened of what might come next, distracted us from giving everything we had to the present.

All Right So Far

Knee or brain? Brain-wise, Carl had been advised at his latest appointment at Toronto Western that he would only need to go to Toronto if his doctor thought it necessary. My driving skills were limited and the stress of finding drivers to go to the city had been getting to us, so we welcomed this decision having no idea that the doctor would totally lose track of Carl. In fact, Carl rarely saw the same doctor more than once, being passed from one doctor to another like a football. Pretty well all his symptoms, the latest Toronto doctor had said, were related to the brainstem. The vision changes which came and went might have to do with blood flow through the brainstem. Poor balance was a given. He fell off the deck one night and emerged with only a black eye. The scary thing is that just a few feet further he could have gone into the ravine and nobody would have missed him for hours.

Carl was deeply sad about the loss of physical abilities but continued to do as much work with his partner Rick as he could. Any task which could be done in a sitting position fell to Carl. At home there were no medical trips to Toronto in the near future and we shifted the brain condition to a back burner in our minds, looking for something fun Carl might do. A change of TV satellite brought in the aviation channel. From every room in the house I overheard shows about planes while Carl slept in front of the TV. What was all this sleeping about anyway? Physical? Emotional? Who could know?

Often, while Carl slept I e-mailed friends and penpals. I needed someone to share my daily life with. From a letter to a friend, mid-November:

> *The Sun Times article about my book launch came out last night, with photos showing my under-eye bags and saying "Balls said this" and "Balls said the other." The young man asked wonderful questions and I like the quotes he chose. Michael now wants to know what to tell my 'adoring fans'. We actually had two calls already so my nose is up in the air with my own importance.*

I went 'red-hatting' recently with lunch at the Three Friends Cafe in Wiarton. When I confided that I felt self-conscious walking down the street in my purple red hat outfit, fourteen women walked me to my car. This gave me the confidence to drive all the way home in my red hat ('til the wind blew it off).

You wonder how Carl is doing? Pain takes much of his attention. And I see a lot of emotional distress, including a few compulsive behaviours.

Away from the house with Rick, Carl concentrated on the task at hand and left no room for fear to creep in. But at home he often withdrew into an understandable place of pain and grief. I tried to appear stoic. But inside I fretted and brooded.

"I should be used to this by now. I should have learned how to separate from Carl's pain," I scolded myself. My copy of Thomas Moore's book, *Care of the Soul*, always seemed to offer comforting words: 'We may have to enter the confusion of another's soul with no hope of ever finding clarity, without demanding that the other be clear in his feelings, and without the hope that one day this person will grow up and get better or express himself more plainly.'

"Do I have the strength to do this?" I asked in my journal. The child in me cried: "It's not fair. I face my own hurt. I can't face his." Underneath I understood that pain comes from the past and staying in the here and now was the answer. "If it never gets any better will we be okay?" I asked, and the answer came: "Yes. Trust."

Messages

January is a great month for lighting candles in the late afternoon. And a great month for snuggling under quilts and dreaming. Catherine told us from her studies in anthropology that at this time of year, people in northern climates want to hibernate or cocoon due to the lack of sun and the cold temperatures.

Winter meant Carl spent more time at home. This was the balance I had longed for, asked for, needed. We ate our suppers in candlelight, not at the dining room table but in chairs by the stove, enjoying that special warmth that seems to come only from wood fires.

I did not mind shoveling ashes out of the stove, dumping them into the black coal scuttle and donning my tall used-to-be-white winter boots to take ashes outdoors. I did not even mind the trek to the woodpile buried under four feet of white. In good weather I wore a path between it and the porch where I built a higher stack for stormy days.

E-mails from friends and pen pals helped with feelings of isolation. So amidst this endless snow the computer was a help. Or was it? In the woods, the internet connection was dial-up all the way, and some messages could be long, especially those with pictures. In one case a publisher who sometimes used my essays sent me his entire magazine each month. I looked forward to hearing from friends but was never sure what was coming in or how long a time it might take.

One snowy morning I checked my e-mail, and where it usually said "receiving 1 of 3 messages" I found out there were six hundred e-mails arriving. Six hundred? Sure enough, as fast as I could hit the delete button more arrived to replace them. Catherine later asked in horror, "Mom, you didn't try to delete just one at a time did you?" Thankfully, no. But the messages were mixed in with things I wanted to keep, and even erasing twenty or so at a time it took more than half an hour and I lost a few of the keepers.

We got quite a variety of Spam in the Not-so-Deep Woods. It came from interesting people like Anatoli Finkelstein and Crystal Barnstormer. I asked Michael about the weird names. "A computer selects names at random from a couple of lists and matches a first and last name," he explained. Well, at least there isn't some poor unfortunate child, saddled from birth with a name like Hezekiah MacTavish.

"And how did they get our address?" I asked my son. Well, it seems that even if you fill out a survey for the TV Guide, or fill in your address in a chat room (wouldn't you think you were safe with Oprah?) the names and addresses could be passed along. Most of the messages informed us about virus protection, but there were also financial offers and inquiries about enlarging varied and sundry parts of our personal anatomy.

At least we have grown up with advertising. We know from experience how to filter messages coming into our homes, but for people new to our country, advertising can be bewildering. I remember a dozen years ago, trying to explain to a newly arrived immigrant child that she and her mother, who owned so few possessions, had not won the huge cash prize promised in the letter delivered to their house that morning. "But look!" she waved the brown envelope with red lettering painted garishly across the front: "Congratulations!" Empty promises to capture the imagination of a mother and child who had managed to cross the world and learn a new language but did not yet understand the intricacies of our commerce-driven culture. I had to tell a little girl who slept on the floor because they did not own a bed, that the promises were a sham.

And now, sitting in front of my own computer, with the wind howling outside the window, I was the one who needed to learn about advertising. Not that I was likely to rush out through the snow and contract for a loan with some unknown lender or have any part of my body enlarged. But for my own protection, I needed to understand more about these messages coming in. I just hoped I would never again get six hundred at one time.

Sex and Violence

Carl says there is not enough sex and violence in my books. He says this for shock value. Carl loves to take people by surprise. He especially loves to take me by surprise. The real surprise is how taken aback people who know me would be if they thought I was writing about sex and violence. Yet any life has these two elements in it. Life is more than smelling roses. More than scrubbing pots. More even than looking into one another's eyes and baring our deepest wounds.

Violence in our life has been limited. There was the burglary at the North Acre. The door to the workshop was mutilated with a large axe, our own. The thief sheltered in the stairwell unseen and apparently unheard from the road. He stole a few items, things he could carry on foot. Not even five hundred dollars worth when you count the value only in money. But he stole our trust too, our feeling that we lived in a safe neighbourhood where no one would intentionally harm us. He left footprints on the living room rug and a bad taste in our mouths. We were pretty sure we knew who the thief was, and we felt a violence done to us even if financially speaking, little damage was done. You do feel violated, when someone breaks down your door, walks around in your home and takes what you thought was yours.

Still, violence is worse when it comes from within the home. There have been a few fights where we said mean things, and one where we were out of control, yelling at one another, and Carl, whose deepest core is gentle, is so ashamed that he shoved me one time. But that is the limit of the violence in our married life. And little other violence has affected us unless you consider the horrible ranting letters a former neighbour used to leave in our mailbox. To us that felt the most violent of all, because all that bitterness and anger, illogical though it was, and apparently the product of an incoherent rage, was directed at us personally, designed to hurt ... and it did.

So we come to sex, which is for me the most private part of my life. This is mine ... ours. I hush Carl when he makes outrageous comments in front of friends. He says: "You think people don't know we have a sex life? You think they look at our kids and figure it was an immaculate conception?" I laugh because I know on one level he is right. But I have not really learned to talk about sex with anyone other than him.

To me, our love life is held close and cherished, and I am selfish enough not to want to share it. All I know is ... young people might think they have a monopoly on sex. They are wrong. It has the potential of getting richer and deeper with the passing years, especially if your partner brings with him, a sense of wonder and tenderness. That's what my partner has brought to our marriage ... a sense of wonder and tenderness, and it is no small gift.

Love Poem from a Woman of a Certain Age

This time of life when there's so little sleeping,
Tired, dreamless, spent with weeping
Safety's found in arms which enfold me,
Pleasure me, treasure me, comfort and hold me.
You are my place of rest and I am wholly blessed.

Broken Places

I was into the baking chocolate again. Any legitimate source of chocolate, the Valentine's chocolate creams, the jersey milk bar out of my purse, being long gone, I resorted to a semi-sweet square you could almost break your teeth on ... a minor satisfaction on a day where I was at loose ends. I loaded the dishwasher and washed the kitchen floor and tried to fill out some paperwork which seemed beyond me. Both players on *The Price is Right* lost. I tried to tell myself it was just that kind of a day.

But who was I kidding? There was nothing commonplace in my lack of focus. Nothing ordinary in any of our recent days. Carl's worsening health frightened me. Weepy weekends happened from time to time when Carl's sense of loss became more than he could bear.

"This isn't yours. I'm burdening you."

"You can't do this by yourself. The least I can do is listen."

I felt helpless a lot of the time. I needed, we needed, understanding people around us. The stress level in our lives had been high for a long time. Did our friends realize how powerless and out of control we felt? Did they know that we only asked for support when we were running short of resources? I wrote letters to family in which my desperation was couched in terms like 'missing you' and 'hope to see you soon'. But in reality the message was: 'Please help. We are so scared. We need to see you in order to reassure ourselves that we are still here and we are still us.' How could I say that?

One Sunday afternoon as we prepared supper for company, there was a frightening and unexpected manifestation of Carl's worsening condition. As he stood at the sink running water he grew troubled. "Who is this person in my kitchen? What is she doing here?"

His confusion deepened. He kept chopping the vegetables for the salad, but the questions in his mind would not let him be: "Where is Sheila? How is she getting here?"

In fact, I was the person in his kitchen. I had been standing at his side absorbed in my own supper preparations. But for those few minutes he did not recognize me. He kept this scary fact to himself until the company left, putting on his 'brave' face and trying so hard to look like his 'old self'. He even managed for those few hours to fool me. But later we lay on the bed as he explained what had happened. There was much weeping, and no one slept much that night.

My struggle to tell people enough to keep them aware of our situation but not enough to scare them away felt like dancing on a tightrope. Wrapped up in their own lives, facing who knows what problems of their own, a couple of people I counted on being there just disappeared from our life, and this hurt Carl who had always been the first to rush to anyone else's assistance. "Wasn't I always kind to people?" he asks me. And "Why am I never invited?"

He tried so hard to look normal and it took everything he had to act like the man he used to be. It broke my heart to see people distance themselves from him. I had trouble figuring out how much truth anyone could handle, how *real* we could be without scaring people so that they would back away from us. And yet, if you aren't *real* is there a friendship there at all? I began to see that looking to others for support can make you even more vulnerable than you were to begin with. Maybe the only thing harder than managing your own frailties, is managing those of someone else at the same time.

> Journal entry Mar 8/03:
> How vulnerable you allow yourself to be with another person seems to be in direct proportion to what you get from the relationship. But there are some people you cannot show weakness to, and times you cannot show your needier side even to friends you trust a great deal. Carl is my 'safe place' and I am his. But I continually seek the same kind of depth and connection he and I feel, with friends. It is hard to find but I am not giving up.

All Right So Far

There were the committed ones of course. The Cathys who in the midst of their own grief still asked about yours. The Donnas who fretted about whether they could keep in touch with you while on their holiday, on the chance you might need them. The Ruths who lugged huge bags of discarded music books all the way home from Florida just in case you might want any of it. The sisters-in-law who responded to your notes, one with offers of support, the other saying repeatedly that she loved you.

With the early days of March, woodpile buried beneath many feet of snow, winter had worn us down. Every few days one of us made a half-hearted effort to dig out a few logs to keep the home fires burning, but it seemed a losing battle. The car, though old and heavily laden with miles (308,000 km to be exact) faithfully started even at thirty-five below, allowing us to get out to pick up the odd quart of milk or make a quick trip to the church, but more important, it let us bring back to one another whatever we experienced and learned. All our lives we liked to come home to one another with little things to share. It saddens me to see so many marriages where people seem to turn away from rather than towards one another, the living of parallel lives replacing the intimacy which could be there ... maybe used to be there.

I watched marriages around me, wondering "How can the partners in these side-by-side relationships heal one another's broken places? How can they feel loved?" For me the world was a place to explore love and trust and forgiveness. Then I would bring what I saw back to my husband/friend to discuss, hoping to learn and where needed, to mend our own marriage. I hoped that in some smaller way, I was also taking what I learned within my marriage, back into the larger world. There was a difference though. Lately I was more guarded. The world was no longer a safe place. Personal issues were harder to share with friends than with my husband. And yet, that turning towards which I treasured within my closest relationship was something I also sought outside of it.

There were days when I felt lonely enough to pick up the address book and leaf through, calling one friend after another to see if anyone would meet me for hot chocolate. I could turn towards enough to ask for a get together, but when I would get a "sorry but …" response I could not bring myself to say "Look, I am really lonely and I need a friend right now." How could I weigh their needs of the moment against my own? It did not mean that my needs were unworthy, or that I did not deserve to have my needs considered and met. But when friend after friend had no time to share, asking became a risky business.

> In my journal I wrote:
> I must learn not to tie my self-worth to the responses of others, even others I love. I am worthy. It is okay to state my feelings and to ask for what I need. And what was it that I needed? Clarity in my thinking. Compassion in my approach to others, the reassurance that there would be good company walking the hard road with us. Above all, the understanding that it sometimes takes darkness to make the light stand out, and that we were learning through our pain to respond and connect in deeper ways.

Maybe I also needed to get out to that woodpile and dig through the layers of snow. There was wood, and therefore warmth, under there somewhere. And in those less safe relationships, what lay buried? Was I brave enough to dig there as well?

Long Winter

Although Wiarton Willie, local weather-predicting groundhog, had promised an early spring, night temperatures were dipping to thirty-five below, concerning since yet another 'Kitty Outside' had taken up residence on our veranda. We knew the drill by now. Every fall the cute little kitten picked up at Keady market last Canada Day to amuse the kids over the summer, grew up and was not quite so cute any more. When the kids went back to school, City-Mom or City-Mom's boyfriend, or both of them, loaded the summer entertainment cat in the car and went for a drive to the country. "There's a barn," we imagined them saying. "He'll be fine there. Lots of mice to eat. Hay bales to keep him warm." And they pitched the little guy out by the side of the road. "He ran away," they would tell the offspring later.

Did they know the barn was old and cold and rickety? Not a hay bale in sight. Did they know the little animal they sent off to catch mice would come close to starving if he didn't freeze first?

We had seen them all, ginger tabby to sleek black, wary of people and bone-thin after a winter living off the land. The tracks in the snow were a giveaway that we had feline company again, but so was the behaviour of our own cats, racing from one window to the next, leaping on top of furniture to get a better look at the intruder.

As had happened far too many winters in the past, David and Cathy once again lent us their live trap and we opened a tin of sardines to put inside. It took a week or so to trap him (just as he learned to trust us ... it felt awful in a way). It was expensive to keep taking strays to the shelter at $38.00 a piece, but my heart went out to the poor creatures on freezing nights. Getting up to the bathroom my eyes invariably turned to the door where one of our cats sat on the mat eighteen inches from the stray on the other side of the door. But where our cat was warm and dry, Kitty Outside had no shelter from the freezing night air.

"At least this one is a male," I told Catherine, "no kittens." She looked at me in disbelief: "Who do you think got the last cat pregnant?" This one was very timid but would make a good pet for someone once he was neutered and could learn to trust people again. At the shelter they told me that the previous one (The Midnight Kitty as we called her) had gone to a farm in the Port Elgin area, so we now knew she was safe. Our pampered indoor cats, curled up by the fire, watched snow pelt the window panes. They had no idea how lucky they were.

It was time to contact family members regarding our annual ice-out contest. Predicting what day we would finally see water from the window, instead of ice, provided a small distraction each March. But compared to Mary, who lived across the road from us during our years at the North Acre, we were strictly amateurs in the sport of creating diversions. Mary once rushed into our house the first week of January, hugging everyone. "Happy Epiphany!" she cried, "I just put up my tree." Since it was the day most of us were taking down our Christmas trees, we were somewhat startled. For the next few weeks we took peeks from the car window when passing Mary's place: "Is it still there?"

So if anyone knew how to liven up a long winter it was Mary. She looked for the positive wherever it could be found and her reward for such an attitude seemed to be that she always looked ten years younger than her current age. She loved the idea that the digits in her phone number were the same as my birthday and even after we moved from the neighbourhood she often called in June with best wishes.

Now it was Mary's birthday and a mutual friend, Liz, planned a gathering to celebrate. People crowded into Liz's living room, stepping over snow boots on the floor, handing over their coats and scarves and mittens. As the large crowd was about to begin dinner, Liz asked us to join hands and she put a CD on to play a song which Mary thought of as a blessing. *This has been a long winter*, the words rang out, and the song went on to say that despite that long winter *there was you*. At each repetition of this line Mary would look at the crowd around her and say "all of you". We were almost through our long winter with April only a day away. And Mary was so clearly delighted to have her friends around her. As blessings go, this song was a perfect fit for this occasion and this time in my life.

Everywhere you went people grumbled about the length and severity of this particular winter. I had felt unwell for much of it. A month of dizzy spells came on gradually and disappeared just as gradually, but not before scaring everyone into thinking I might have had another stroke. As the dizzy spells receded, a burning pain ran from my right shoulder around under the right breast. The doctor pronounced it "dry skin". It turned into shingles, but fortunately the mildest case possible.

Thankfully Carl had experienced no further scares since his sudden severe memory loss. Cathy suggested that with his strange sleep habits, we should think of it as a waking dream, and this made sense to me. Cathy was always helping to make sense of things which troubled me. It had been seven months now since a tragic accident took their son, and we were seeing her and David a couple of times a month, but it was hard to tell who was supporter and who was supported, which seems to me like an okay basis for a friendship.

If the winter had seemed long to us, how much longer must it have seemed to the Grahams? Thanksgiving, Christmas, Valentine's Day ... each one spent with an empty chair at the holiday table.

Taming the Bear

For Catherine's end of March birthday I gave her a book I had been writing since January. Catherine had been working for the Ministry of Natural Resources, unlikely to see wildlife near her tall many-windowed building. But she had heard me complain of occasional nervousness when I stopped in the woods after dark to unlatch the gate to our property. So I had called the book Back Away Slowly, referring to her instructions to me regarding the meeting of bears out in the woods, a particularly unlikely event at this time of year.

I watched my daughter leaf through the book murmuring words and phrases aloud, and pausing to smile at certain points. She knew immediately where the title had come from and laughed at the little bear brooch I had attached to the cover. Funny and loveable, the wide-eyed shaggy figure looked nothing like bears in our area. "Oh, I will wear this to work," she exclaimed.

I had enjoyed the trip down to Guelph, since three hours further south meant less snow than we had at home. For me, even without the added discomfort of a six-month winter, my moods were unpredictable. I was coming off Premarin after several years. Some women sailed through menopause without a hitch. I was not one of them. A few years earlier our neighbour had joked that she could tell time by watching me endure hot flashes. Every four minutes: sweater off. Next four minutes: sweater on. At night it was worse, with covers thrown aside frequently and night sweats requiring a change of nightgowns.

Carl and I had watched as Doctor Phil, king of daytime TV talk shows and guru of troubled families, joked with the husband of a menopausal woman: "Your experience might be compared to having a grizzly bear in the garage, and being told to go out and hug the bear."

This became a watchword in our marriage at tense times, those flashpoints where a fight might break out. For these difficult years, could Carl just 'hug the bear'?

A woman I knew had inherited her ex-husband's naturopathic textbooks. No matter what ailed you, this lady had the cure at her fingertips. "Take your calcium at night," she insisted, "not in the morning. And give progesterone cream a try."

Advice on Taming the Bear

"Progesterone," she told me, "will calm the nerves and hold thee
some cooler in the body and quieter in the mind.
And then as dark surrounds you and sleeplessness has found you,
your calcium pill at nightfall should ease your soul in kind."

And these small alterations would offer transformations
to soothe the grizzly bear who raged where hormones undermined
my previous composure, and offer up some closure
to stormy sensitivities of the unconscious mind.

"Do other couples fight like we do?" Carl asked me one day. "We only have one fight, I decided. Unfortunately, we have it over and over." I picked up a copy of Thomas Moore's book *Soulmates*. 'When trouble arrives, we think the relationship itself is open to doubt,' said the introduction, and, 'Pain and difficulty can sometimes serve as the pathway to a new level of involvement.' You got that right, Thomas. But how I wished we could find an easier and wiser pathway. The hormone thing was enough of a struggle, especially when added in on top of the interminable cold and snow outside. Could we not find our way to deeper intimacy without fighting?

Dear Carl:

When there is an upset, can I just tell you I am distressed by 'old issues' and turn to you for comfort and skip all the exchange of "who-hurt-who-when"? I still think If we could focus only on feelings and needs, we would repair the damage faster than we do when we stir up all the rubble and kick it around.

I find that it takes me months of knowing something intellectually, before I can know it emotionally. When I am ready, opportunities to let go of some confining belief usually crop up everywhere. They don't feel like opportunities at the time though. They feel like hurt and anxiety. It takes careful attention to see why I am stuck in some negative flight pattern. Seeing myself in a fixed role limits me, and those closest to me. What is the advantage to being 'the strong one' or 'the victim' or 'the leader' or any number of other roles I might choose?

I think marriage lets us practice ways to connect more deeply in the world. On the plus side, Carl and I have learned about balancing our own, and one another's needs and to talk about that honestly. We have learned what motivates us and what sacrifices we are willing to make. Less happily we've seen that in our unfortunate urge to show we are right, we too often give up possibilities for contented times together to prove a point. We have allowed anxiety to get in control when our minds cautioned reason.

> *Dear Carl:*
> *You came home yesterday to find me in one of my 'same old-same old' fearful places. But this time you saw that it was about me, not about you. Thank you for loving me through it so that I could put aside some of the heavy baggage to begin healing an old issue. I need to learn from that, and if I see myself seeking safety rather than peace of mind, need to admit that in order to help keep our connection honest and open. You deserve the sense of peace of knowing it is 'about me/not about you'.*

The old fear-laden issues were like tattered suitcases I had been dragging along behind me. They slowed me down and filled my hands so that I could not carry something more worthwhile. They were not in any way attractive, and nobody else would want to look at them. But those who love me, do look at them, and likely wish I would drop that heavy baggage and move on. With kind listening and careful questions they encourage me to do just that. And isn't it funny? Everybody else's baggage looks just as ratty as your own.

"Why on earth would they choose to drag that around with them?" we ask.

How wonderful to think that I was married to a man willing to look past my ratty suitcases and go out to the garage and hug the bear.

Encounters

One of our great pleasures as winter ended each year was to feed the thin raccoons just out of hibernation. In front of the sunporch a big tree served as stairway to the buffet we placed there on a small bench. The first night we put out our apple wedges and a handful of birdseed and kept the room in darkness. But after a few nights, with lights blazing, both on the deck and in the dining room, we watched the raccoons and they watched us. We sat in rocking chairs gazing at the thin bodies as they stood at the little bench like diners at a soda fountain counter. Always they ate with good manners, nibbling daintily at their apple, looking up from the bench with a few seeds clinging to their noses.

They came for a week or two to fatten up, and then returned to the forest. Had they gone back to bed for a little more sleep or were they somehow able to get food on their own? We only knew that we looked forward every March to this end-of-winter entertainment.

One year a Mama raccoon we had known as a youngster, returned with four babies, her face situated in the middle of the group as if arranged for the photograph I only wished I could have taken.

We had expected to see far more wild animals in the forest than we ever actually did. More often we saw wildlife on our way to and from town. I wrote to Carl's sister to describe a one of a kind encounter with a fox.

All Right So Far

Good Morning Helen,

In your last e-mail you mentioned that you had not heard my fox story? This happened just before Carl got sick. I was on the outskirts of town on my way home and as I rounded a corner I saw a beautiful fox on my right side running along beside me in the field. His tail streamed out behind him and he looked healthy and happy, just enjoying the sunshine and the breeze. Another car approached, and the fox ran away some distance. When the car had disappeared, the fox came back, this time running close to the car and looking right at me. It felt as if the fox ran beside me for five or six minutes, but when I later returned to that corner I realized it could not have been more than a minute.

That minute felt important to me. So out of curiosity I later asked friends what symbolism the fox might have in native spiritual beliefs, and it was this: the fox is very alert and watchful. It is protective of its family. And so the message I could take from this is 'Guard well your family'. As you know, this was a time in our life when our marriage was running off the rails, and it was a time, though we did not know it yet, that Carl's health was in jeopardy. So I did need to be mindful of my family's 'safety', emotionally and physically.

The reason the fox story came up in the first place was because we had been talking about beautiful encounters with nature. At our neighbour Mary's birthday party, her friend Pat had told me a great nature story. Pat's friend was driving along the highway one day when there was a little thump against the car and she realized a tiny saw-whet owl had flown into the car. She stopped by the roadside and was sad to see the perfect little creature lying there with not a mark on it. Rather than waste its little life, she decided take it to a local wildlife artist who might like to paint it. So she placed the small body on the back seat of the car and drove on.

A minute or two later she heard a small sound, and there was the saw-whet, not dead after all, but perched on the seat just behind her. "I'll turn around and take it back where it came from," she decided, and as she did this, the little bird fluttered first to the dashboard, and then to the steering wheel where it sat regarding her with huge eyes. She reached the spot she was looking for on the road and rolled down the window. Tiny wings moved to perch on the window, round eyes looked at her a final time, and back to its own life the little owl flew.

I remembered how Cathy had described driving on the Bruce Peninsula around the time of her mother's death, when she had an encounter with an eagle looking straight into her eyes. "Strength," said the native elders. "It was giving you strength." There was no way of knowing then, that when my own mother died, birds would also take on a significance for us. Beginning on the morning following her passing we saw orioles everywhere. Catherine felt that her Gram was "sending birds" particularly orioles. Everyone dear to her saw them, even a lady who did not know of her death told me when I called, that for the first time ever she had orioles in the yard.

As Catherine sat weeping on her back steps a morning or two after her Gram's death, a little mourning dove came and sat with her. Then the day after the memorial service a baby seagull showed up and stood in the pouring rain facing our front door waiting patiently. "Is he still there?" Carl would ask each time I walked through the hallway, and each time, he stood, just as before, watching the door.

The funny thing is, I had never liked seagulls. They always made so much noise, boldly interrupting your picnic to scream for food. But this bird stood in silence. I approached him and he did not fly away. He just walked off a pace or two and continued his vigil. Finally I took him a crust of bread. He ate it quietly, then moved off the walkway onto the lawn where he slept for the rest of the evening. In the morning he was gone.

Expecting

I stared at the bunny design on the plate I had just bought. I tried to imagine making cookies with my first grandchild. But it didn't feel real. How could I get Catherine's news to sink in, really sink in. She was pregnant. We were going to be grandparents.

Years earlier I had spent a happy couple of hours with my niece when she was about three. The feeling of that tiny hand in mine was tucked away in a corner of my heart. I remembered the grass blowing, and the sun on our faces, and how I had sung to her as we walked around a field. I tried to imagine looking for minnows down at the dock, a little figure in shorts and sunhat peering into the water. Ah, now I was beginning to really get it. My mother had wanted to be called Gram. Katie had been Grandma. Nana, I determined. I want to be Nana.

I wished I could knit something for the baby. Isn't that what a prospective grandmother was supposed to do? But my knitting career had been short and disastrous. All those years ago I had made two sweaters. One of them fit. More or less. The other was a salmon pink colour in about a size fifty-two. It could have functioned as a dress I suppose, if I had added a belt. Even if I had been a good knitter, and heaven knew that was not the case, my fingers were arthritic now. Gripping a pen was hard enough. Anything as slender as a knitting needle was out of the question.

I liked to look back all those years ago when my fingers worked better and my art had been embroidery work. I brought enough hand worked pillowcases to my marriage to last a lifetime, and indeed many of them did last for decades. Carl and I taught at the same school, and some lunch hours I sat in the staff room stitching an embroidered tablecloth or pillowcase. Staff members teased Carl about a future of waking up with an impression of roses embedded in the side of his face.

I was embroidering a design of royal purple lupins the night I went into labour with Catherine, and I used those pillow slips for company only for a while before deciding to put them away in a drawer to give my daughter someday. Will she give them to her own daughter in the far future? "Your grandmother worked on these the night I was born."

While waiting for Catherine's baby I wanted so much to make a baby gift with my own hands. Bibs are small. Could I manage a bib? Then I remembered the lion and lamb.

Newlyweds in the 1970's did not own and could not afford much art. Carl and I did what we could to decorate the walls of those first homes. This often involved fabric and a cut and paste technique, and on one occasion blue geometric patterns cut from a sheet and glued to black panels which hung from the ceiling in place of a headboard ... not our finest decorating moment.

But not everything we made was 1970's tacky. If there had been an attic in our house I might have looked there for a long lost family treasure. In our yard a discarded truck box served as basement/attic substitute. Sure enough, buried in the truckbox, one piece from those early years had survived, a crewel work lion and lamb in a rough barn board frame.

With artist friend Helen Harrison, Carl surveyed the unfortunate background of olive green. "Why not paint it?" Helen asked. So the lion and lamb stitched by me so many years ago, ended up sitting on a grassy hill in front of a starry sky, these added features painted by Carl, ready for the birth of Liam (William Hugh) Robertson next November twenty-third.

Operation

Carl's knee would be replaced in March and all we needed to do was find a way to get to, and a place to stay, in Toronto. Friends rallied around us, neighbour Ruth offering to drive and Jean from the symphony inviting us to stay in her beautiful home. Carl's day-long pre-op wound up just in time for rush hour. Lanes of traffic weaving in and out were scary to me but Ruth ran one hand through her blonde spiked hair, tossed her leopard skin scarf over one shoulder and remarked: "I always wanted to be a stock car driver."

Jean's home was so huge that when we descended the massive staircase in the morning we had to call out in order to locate one another. The room where we visited after dinner had lots of bookcases and a fireplace along one long wall. Jean's two dogs played wildly in the center of the room and the lively little Jack Russell terrier jumped up and down frightening Jean's old cat.

As far as I could tell, the cat lived on the bookcase. She ate and slept and took little walks up and down the mantel. She must have come down to use her litter box, but for the most part she seemed to live out her little life above the hearth, peering down now and then at the small dog bouncing below. Jean said the cat was probably deaf. Every once in a while, whether in warning or in loneliness, she cried out the loudest meow I had ever heard.

The hospital was not quite awake when we arrived in the early morning. We sat in a silent, darkened waiting room with half a dozen other patients. Were they all as nervous as us? I worried about Carl and the week ahead. He had faced surgeries before, but always in our own familiar town. I would find comfort in going back at the end of the day to Jean's warm personality and gracious home but I had no understanding of what Carl's next few days would be like, physically, or any other way. Once I left Toronto would he be lonely?

Carl later explained how in the large room where he waited to go to the operating room, people wore blue net caps and "those gowns everyone has to fiddle with at the back to make sure they aren't sticking out of." He told me he had felt like an actor in a science fiction movie with everyone walking around in these strange outfits.

Carl arrived from surgery joking with the nurses. Whatever drugs they used left him animated and for the time being without pain. I needn't have worried about him being lonely in the big city. Jack and Helen came for a long visit, taking me back home with them. Dave went down for a couple of days, and two more out of town friends dropped in on the Saturday. Carl hardly had time for physio.

In all the hullabaloo surrounding Carl's surgery I lost track of our customary end of winter family contest. Every year we all chose a date when the ice might depart from the lake. The person closest was granted a Major Award. We borrowed this phrase from a Christmas movie we all enjoyed. In the movie the hero wins a ghastly table lamp in the shape of a woman's leg, with the fringed shade perched atop it as the skirt. To his wife's chagrin he insists on displaying the prize in their living room window.

Our prizes were in fact chosen after the winner was determined, which was one way of being sure to pick something the winner might like. There was one winner, however who was habitually ungracious, always expressing noisy dissatisfaction with our rather modest prizes. "A boat would be a better prize," claimed Carl. "Or a car." Together, Jacqueline and I decided to teach him a lesson. Jacqueline came into my life through our shared interest in writing. She looked a little like a mature version of Anne of Green Gables, without the braids. Her spirit was kind and generous, and she had an imagination to match Anne's as well.

All Right So Far

To All Former Ice-Out Entrants:

Everyone is disappointed at the cancelled Ice-Out Contest this year. So Jacqueline has suggested a new challenge: I am calling it the 'Moo Alley Open' (Daffodil Opening that is!). There has been some discussion as to whether Carl will be allowed to enter as he traditionally accuses the esteemed judge (moi) of cheating. It has been decided that he can enter but may only choose March dates. If disappointed he can console himself by leafing through last year's major award, a photo album stuffed, by Michael and Jacqueline, with Canadian Tire money. So say-eth the judge.

By the time Carl came home, neither ice nor daffodils were to be seen at the lake. Everyone including the robins, thought winter was over but immediately two days of snow set us straight. We also thought life was getting back to normal, but we would have to be set straight about that as well.

Carl was getting stronger, moving around the house sometimes with walker, sometimes with cane, and sometimes unsupported. The dining room table holding our *life* at the moment had no space for friends, so we cleared the nursing supplies and paperwork away long enough to invite Dave and Carol for supper. Then, because the VCR was in our bedroom, Carl and I sat on the bed and tucked our guests into a couple of rocking chairs beside the bed to watch *Pirates of the Carribean*. Laughter was just what we needed to prepare us for the ups and downs of the next few weeks.

From a letter to friends, late March/04:

We are managing the nursing care, appointments etc. but as far as the house goes, Moo Alley is a bit of a sinking ship. I get groceries, cook, do laundry, and manage a bare minimum of cleanliness. The clutter is out of control in some parts of the house (notably the dining room table) but so far I keep the bedroom tidy as a 'safe place' since I am a bit claustrophobic.

The good news: Carl is elated to just 'not feel sick' and be mostly out of pain. Walking is very difficult for him but we made it up to Lion's Head to the doctor Tuesday and will go for a blood test today. Nurses come twice a week and a physio as well. Friends have visited every day so far and this is really cheering Carl up. They all say the same thing: "The old Carl is back".

Do take care, and know that, as one of my favourite sayings proclaims, we are All Right So Far.

from HMCS Moo Alley,
sinking ship,

Sheila.

Part 3

New Directions

The Entertainment

Open the doors and windows and let the fresh air in. Winter is far enough behind us that we finally trust it is spring. We act as if we have been hibernating. We shake ourselves off and invite the world back into our (hopefully) spring-cleaned den. It will be halfway through June before we can safely take the electric blanket off the bed.

Spring brought with it the prettiest birds we had ever seen in our time at the lake, orioles and rose-breasted grosbeaks just outside the kitchen window. We put out feed but the chipmunks ran off with the whole lot of it in short order, breaking our hummingbird feeder in the process. A little female came to the window where I liked to do my writing. She looked in hopefully, wings whirring at a tremendous speed. "I'm so sorry," I told her, "If I put it back up they will only break it again."

Out in the garden I had placed an ornate white tin feeder bought before I understood the intricacies of feeding birds in the woods. I loved the feeder the minute I saw it, and knew it could hang from the tall white hanger left over from Catherine's wedding. It would stand in the corner where we planted tulips last fall.

Last fall I had not understood the facts of life concerning tulip planting in the forest. As soon as there is disturbed earth, the bulbs are dug up in a great hurry, and that is the end of the tulips. Carl and I tried shaping chicken wire into protective cages with five bulbs inside each one but even that experiment had very limited success. At the south end of our little cliff garden, the five surviving tulips bloomed. In mid-garden was one misshapen tulip leaf. Could they have grown down instead of up?

I was bent over examining the single tulip which had come up at the north end beside the new feeder, when all hell broke loose just above my head. Inside the tin lantern feeder is a tall glass tube with a gap at the top maybe an inch high. Apparently a chipmunk can fit through an inch high gap. While I recovered my presence of mind, I watched the flattened furry face press against the tube. I could imagine him crying "Lemme outta here!"

That episode was just a beginning. Soon the striped bandit learned to wrap both paws around the metal hanger and shinny up it like a tiny firefighter going the wrong direction. Not much chance of seed surviving here. "I'm sorry birds. I don't have a lot of choices here."

But if I lost patience with my woodland visitors, I could seek out human company, better behaved and sometimes just as entertaining. One Friday morning I went into town to see my aunt and uncle who were visiting my Mom. "It's so nice of you to come all the way into town to see us," said Uncle Dave. But who wouldn't drive all the way to town to see Uncle Dave's eyes light up when you enter the room? Besides, his remarkable memory for detail produces funny stories no one ought to miss.

That day he told me about the time he was playing in the Scottish pipe band up north. "We always hated those ladies' curling events," he began, "because some of the women would get hammered, and then there was trouble." Uncle Dave explained how the band had been standing at attention on the curling rink when he felt something clutch at his ankle. Looking down, he discovered a lady (well he described her as a lady ... I'm not so sure) sliding along, sort of "doing the backstroke" and peering up the men's kilts. Now I ask you, wouldn't you drive all the way to town to hear a story like that? Funnier than a chipmunk in a bird feeder.

Signs

Signs (re-printed from *Our Side of the Fence*)

The highway is mine alone (or almost alone). There is little traffic this Thursday morning as I speed up the peninsula towards Tobermory. The drive is familiar, the circumstances are anything but! Only a couple of hours ago Carl left to do some work for Dr. Hugh Black. But an unsettling call from Hugh has changed the course of my day: "Carl was just sitting down to have some coffee when he went white as a sheet and became very ill."

An ambulance has taken Carl to the clinic and Helen, his sister who lives close by is already with him. Hugh's voice is calm, and this in turn allows me to be calm. "I'm on my way," I tell him, knowing that this is serious, but not understanding just how serious.

Considering the situation, I am pretty calm. I try to avoid thoughts of the *what ifs* and just concentrate on driving. There is the checkerboard corner Carl and our writer friend Debbie Bauer keep disagreeing about. This is the location according to Carl, while Debbie's corner is a bit further north.

The phrase *north of the checkerboard* is common in these parts. If you are born and raised north of Wiarton you take a lot of good-natured teasing on the subject, as in "You know you're from north of the checkerboard when there are more than twelve trucks lying around in your yard." Carl admits to being from "north of..." although while dating him, I never saw a single truck decomposing in the farmyard. The problem, for Carl, is where, exactly the checkerboard corner is situated, and he and Debbie are of opposing opinions.

I pass the road to Berford Lake where Carl as a teenager used to retreat from the heat of summer haying which he hated so much. There is the workshop where I rehearsed for a CD a few years ago. I hear that the guitar player who lived there, a gentle giant of a man, has since passed away. That brings me back to the present, and my own gentle giant. I don't know much about the clinic at Tobermory. Will there be doctor there, or only nursing staff?

I must have long passed Debbie's checkerboard corner, though I don't know its exact location. I have no idea who is right, but she and Carl are both stubborn. Just a few weeks ago we sat in our dining room as each one listed people who would back up their points of view.

At Ferndale I see the big windmill at the corner where Michael used to turn in for his shift at the factory. The road is long and straight, open to the wind, with deep ditches on either side. It worried me when Michael travelled it in winter. It is no longer a worry since a car accident on a rain-wet highway near Brampton took away his car and therefore his job. He misses the car but I doubt he misses the long drive.

The huge blades of the turbine rotate slowly. They say that if you live nearby you can hear them singing in the wind. They say that if it stops turning, it costs thousands of dollars to re-start. I don't know if any of this is true. But we see the windmill often. Carl comes frequently to work for Hugh and Shirley Black. Helen is their sister in law, and mine too. Living near them means she can see Carl when he is working up there. We also see the windmill whenever we go up to the Northwinds Restaurant for their Sunday buffet. We drove up with Cathy and David just a couple of weeks ago. Over supper, Carl added David to his list of checkerboard supporters. David's grandfather was a local pioneer. Surely that imparts credibility. Are you listening Debbie?

I see the road Carl's mother and I travelled looking for Debbie's book launch last year. I remember Katie saying: "I didn't think it was this far! I didn't think it was this far!" while we drove further and further north.

At least I know how far I must drive today. Hugh has reminded me where the clinic is located, and as I pass Crane River, I know I am getting within range. Minutes later I spot the flowerpot structure which announces Tobermory ahead. There is the clinic on the left.

The office is empty and patients in the waiting room look at me curiously. Prior to June, the clientele here is almost exclusively restricted to locals. I wait. Then I sit. Then I go down a long hall and see that the receptionist is making coffee. I return and sit for two more minutes, then think: "Nuts to this. I want to see my husband." I go down the hall again and this time, announce myself to the receptionist. "Follow me," she says, and leads me even further back in the building.

Carl is surrounded by people and machines. He has constant attention, which means the people waiting in the other part of the building will continue waiting for a while. His pulse, it seems, was two-hundred and seventy when the ambulance arrived. In moving him through the kitchen door, the attendants bumped the stretcher and the jolt slowed his heart rate down. Did this save his life?

Helen and I sit on two chairs at the far end of the large room giving the doctor and nurse space to work in. A small black box advertises Carl's pulse rate. While it has dropped significantly from the two-seventy, it never goes lower than a hundred and forty something.

Doctor Thompson is friendly and matter-of-fact. He and Nurse Dorothy work like a tag team seeming to anticipate one another's next move and adjust with little conversation.

Before I arrived, Carl had passed out and awakened to find Dorothy standing over him with the paddles, ready to shock him back to life. Carl asked if there were alternatives. The doctor explained that he would try a drug which might stop Carl's heart from beating. Carl would be 'dead' and then 'come back'.

Tears roll down my face. Carl's rare brain condition means there are so many unknowns. Am I seeing him alive for the last time? Helen puts her arm around my shoulders and closes her eyes. She is praying. So am I, but I want my eyes open.

They give the injection. No obvious change. Carl remains fully conscious. "Did you feel anything?" asks the nurse. "I felt a bit funny," Carl answers. We continue to watch the monitor. No change. Calls go back and forth between Doctor Thompson and the hospital in Owen Sound. They will send Carl down by ambulance. I take his belongings and a bag of cheese and crackers Helen has gathered together, retracing my journey back south. I do not even notice the checkerboard corner this time. My mind lingers with husband and children, and how to break the news of Carl's condition, especially to Catherine, newly pregnant and fighting constant nausea.

Several days in hospital and many tests later, doctors found a blood clot which was the probable source of the trouble. Daily I visited, and came home to e-mails from friends offering the strength I needed. My favourite came from Debbie: "tell him if it helps keep his pulse down, he can have the checkerboard wherever he wants."

>Postscript:
>Carl's Mom came to visit the other day. She brought Carl a chicken and a pineapple and a piece of exasperating news: There were two checkerboards, but when it comes right down to locating the original checkerboard ... Debbie is right! The checkerboard wars are over.

A Little Drama Here and There

"Carl's on the phone," someone called across the church kitchen. Despite Carl's close call the week before, we had not yet come to a place where emergencies were a way of life. No worries crossed my mind as I tossed the dishcloth into the sink and took the receiver: "I put the truck in the ditch. Hit a hydro pole. I don't even know what happened. I just blacked out."

We were down to a single vehicle but then we were also down to a single driver. "If I were you," the doctor had advised, "I'd pay a fine for careless driving and stay out from behind the wheel until we get new medications working and your health is more stable. Careless driving may be an embarrassing charge, but it's a lot harder to get a license back if they take it away for medical reasons."

So I drove. Carl took new pills. The reasons for his blackout remained a mystery, but in a day or two his body began providing clues. We lay on the bed one evening with Carl trying to make sense of the strange sensation he was noticing: "It's like a fish flopping around in my chest," he explained. This was our first of many trips to hospital, with me plotting out the route which had the fewest traffic lights, and Carl insisting there was no reason for speed.

We began making this drive regularly and joked that these excursions to hospital were our regular romantic night out. Before long we skipped the triage process altogether as we were usually spotted by a nurse just inside the glass doors: "Need to see a doctor Carl?" and in a flash we were zipped past the rows of waiting patients. Carl's previously strong heart had suddenly gone out of control.

We lived twenty minutes from the nearest hospital and thirty from a center with a heart specialist. And we were having far too many of these not-so-romantic date-nights. Finally after four or five episodes Carl was admitted. I did not envy the nurses their job. Carl may have been sick, but he felt well. And a bored Carl is not a happy Carl.

I visited daily, heading back to the lake in the early evenings. Often when the forest around the house was already dark, the bright meadow beckoned and with journal in hand, I sat on a log reflecting on the sudden changes in our life.

Once Carl had spent the better part of a week in hospital, they used paddles to re-set his heart. "It won't be like on TV," the staff assured us. "It looks violent on programs like ER where they have to hurry because of sudden situations, but here where we are prepared in advance, it's a much calmer process."

Three days later the hospital discharged Carl with still more changed medications and a litany of new instructions. I longed to see a *whole* Carl again, rather than 'Carl-the-patient'. There was no whole Sheila either. I wanted to be strong but lacked focus and energy. The arthritis in my fingers plagued me daily.

Crouched between the deck and the narrow band of earth, which bordered the cliff in front of the house, I tucked plants into the earth, wondering all the while "How deep should they go? How far apart should they go?" Carl had always been the gardener. But if he was stuck in hospital, I would try to do the things he would have done.

My mind wandered between Carl at home, my church job where I was feeling burnt out, and Guelph where my pregnant daughter had been labeled *pre-diabetic* just as they packed to move. She wasn't lifting heavy boxes was she? Where I used to imagine a pot on the stove to put my worries in and move to the back burner, I thought I might need to create a new image: a whole suitcase to store away in the attic of my brain. In my journal I wrote, 'Send in the clowns God. Nothing seems funny anymore.'

How did this happen? There I was, going along in life feeling reasonably capable, when so many new and scary circumstances were piled onto my outstretched arms, I began to stagger under the unexpected weight.

Over the course of our lives we have often followed friend Bonnie's advice: "Don't say 'I can't.' Say instead, 'I could if.' and let someone else handle the ifs." There were people who would help me with the ifs. But I needed to change my thinking to "Show me how I can." I picked up a pencil and drew a funny little stick figure. It didn't even have hair. Just a sad face and shaky looking legs. Surrounding it I wrote points of advice to myself: Notice that you are growing stronger. Lean on a friend if you need to. Ask someone else to carry one of the weights for a while. See that you will learn from all this, to be more compassionate with others.

July tenth we went up to Lion's Head for a medical appointment. The appointment was to check what was happening with Carl's heart but Carl's full attention was concentrated on an ugly wart on his finger. He was determined to get rid of it. The young doctor serving for the summer holiday listened to Carl's pulse. "You go to the hospital right now."

"But what about my wart?" Doctor G tilted his head to one side and furrowed his eyebrows at Carl: "The wart doesn't matter. Go now."

"It matters to me. I want it off." Reluctantly, Dr. G. treated the wart. "Will. You. Go. Now?"

The doctor arrived in the emergency ward practically on our heels, just minutes after we registered. He was clearly worried. There were whispered conferences with a second doctor and phone calls to Owen Sound. "We are going to have to shock your heart again," they concluded.

An hour passed. It seemed to be taking forever to get the process started. I wandered around outdoors trying to keep a distance, but with its being such a small hospital I could see and hear through the open window to Carl's room. "These doctors are so young," I thought. "How experienced are they?"

When Carl had gone through this procedure in the Grey Bruce Regional Health Center the calm and organization had been comforting. But this was an unplanned procedure performed far from a city hospital.

We knew no one in Lion's Head but I made a quick call to update friends who responded by jumping into their cars and coming straight to the hospital. We sat on the floor in the hallway, talking quietly, and I thought: "What a strange place for my friends to be introduced to one another."

I would not see Carl after the procedure. The second doctor came out to the hall, explaining Carl must go to Owen Sound right away. Kind young Dr. G. would ride with Carl in the ambulance. "Leave now," my friends advised, "and you can be there at the hospital when they bring him in." Racing down highway 6, I was passed by the ambulance. Thank heavens no lights were flashing. No sirens were wailing. But I wept anyway.

Carl was settled when I reached the GBRHC and we ended our tumultuous day quietly enough. Our last meal had been an early lunch but meals and times and normal routines had been far from my mind. Finally, leaving the hospital around nine-thirty that night I picked up Chinese food to take back to the lake, wishing only that Carl could share it with me.

> Journal entry July 15/04
> Carl came home late Sunday afternoon with a urinary tract infection added to the mix. His knee pain continues and Cathy is convinced that the increased pain is connected to the recent heart complications.

Through Carl's illness our daughter had asked "Should we come home?" and I told her no. The decision to travel two and a half hours with pregnancy sickness would have been a tough one for her. And I did not want to admit to her or even to myself how ill Carl had been. Calling family home was a step I could not fathom taking.

A few days later, Cathy, in her tactful way pointed out some truths to me. That's what good friends do. They tell you the truth in a way you can bear to hear it. "Was it a good decision to be 'protecting' Catherine at a time when you needed her and her father could have died?"

I knew Cathy was gently guiding me to a better balance. I hoped I would do better next time. I hoped there would be no next time.

One Cow Running

Journal entry Aug. 13/04:

> Why is Carl's knee still so painful? Should it not be healing? Today his physiotherapist phoned the doctor's office out of concern: "I won't work with this man anymore until he has more help." The knee pain frustrated Carl so that he was frequently upset.

"I'm useless," he complained. "I go to jobs with Rick but there's hardly anything I can do anymore. I lose my balance. My hands don't work right."

"Can you keep your focus on the things you can still do?"

"Don't lecture me."

"When you give me advice, is that lecturing?"

"Yes."

I disagreed but let it go. It wasn't worth arguing over. Despite a personality, which tended towards mood swings Carl had nevertheless always been a logical thinker. Now he seemed to stop thinking things through and became reactive in the extreme. One evening after he had felt unwell for a couple of days I asked "Do you think you might have a virus?" I was flabbergasted when he reacted in hurt and anger:

"What are you accusing me of?"

"I'm not accusing you of anything. I just wondered if you're catching something."

"You think I'm lazy."

"That is nothing like I said. I asked about your health."

I walked away before he could say anything further. Giving him a short cool down period and then a hug defused the situation but this was the second of such incidents in a short time. All his life Carl had struggled with feeling blamed when things went wrong. Was he getting ready to face this issue? If so, did this mean I could expect regular outbursts as some kind of test to see if I loved him anyway? This must be what Thomas Moore meant when he spoke of entering "the confusion of another's soul."

Through the early autumn I might have become preoccupied with the changes in Carl, except that life held distractions to keep me busy. My mother moved from her little white house to a senior's apartment building. Michael began selling his sterling silver jewelry designs at an Art Co-op. We managed a vacation to Mackinac Island, our beautiful little grandson was born, and I rediscovered yoga.

It had been quite a long time since the years I had attended yoga classes. By this time I was unquestionably a lapsed yoga student. My waist wouldn't turn. My arms were weak. When I bent over my fingers came nowhere near the floor. If my instructor Riejanne were to see the shape my body was in, she would be horrified.

Now that alone was an un-yoga-like thought. Riejanne would accept me where I was and encourage me just to do what I could reasonably do. "Listen to your own body," she used to say. I was listening. But I didn't like what I heard. A few months ago I had begun hearing the whimpers and whines of a body in trouble.

For most of my life I have struggled with pain in my low back and my neck. When Carl and I took to the roads on snowmobiles in our early marriage I marveled at how he could swivel his neck around to check on where I was and whether I was okay. My own neck refused to turn even half that far.

Riejanne's sharp eyes watched her students, picking out where the injuries were and adjusting the positions to make them safe. She studied me as I did exercises in her yoga class: "You have a neck injury. Keep your head bent," she cautioned. Towards the end of each class she tiptoed about the room where students lay stretched out on their mats. To people like me she delivered a chair, placing it under our feet to protect the lower back.

As class came to an end each week, Riejanne's soothing voice led us to relax, urging us to empty our minds of busy details we might be harbouring: "If thoughts do enter your mind," she encouraged, "just let them pass by." Her voice lived on in my head. "Listen to your body."

About a year ago, frequent back spasms sent me to the chiropractor's office I lay mostly on my front, eyes down, but I did not need eyes to sense the shaking of her head in dismay. Something must be done about my deteriorating body. I searched the television for a yoga class and found one which might work.

Even a dozen years after my last yoga class, I valued Riejanne's unhurried pacing. This TV class went at a bewildering speed for me. But it was only half an hour long and the instructor spoke in gently soothing tones. The class was arranged with a warm-up, a twelve minute lesson, and a relaxation time at the end. Each section ended with the word Namaste which serves as a combination greeting/blessing.

After a day or two the word 'Namaste' let me predict exactly when loud commercials would interrupt, and by keeping the TV remote close, I could hit it at strategic moments, continuing to stretch and breathe through the commercials, or, if pressed for time, slip out to run the bathwater just before relaxation. I suspect no yoga teacher on earth would condone that kind of multi-tasking.

I chose to practice yoga in a five foot space next to my bed. I folded a quilt into four to offer some padding and lay it down diagonally. Most days both cats arranged themselves along the edge of the bed in order to keep an eye on the proceedings. This is an improvement on the last television class I did about fifteen years ago. There I had the entire family room to myself but on either side of the room a child was getting ready for school, and Nickie my long-haired black cat thought it most exciting that I was positioning myself at floor level. Frequently he would step onto my stomach or chest and either walk the length of my body or settle himself to gaze into my eyes. Riejanne taught us to do yoga with eyes closed but how do you keep them closed when a cat climbs onto your belly?

With this TV class I kept my eyes open. I liked the background scenery for one thing. It switched magically between beautiful outdoor locations and a tidy spacious studio. There was little enough of *tidy* and *spacious* in my bedroom. It also helped me to watch the students on the screen because I had forgotten much about the positions and needed to see again how to do them. As it was, I lost my balance and toppled over from time to time.

I've always liked the cat position. On hands and knees I can maintain my balance. And the child pose is soothing, bending forward to stretch out the usually aching back. For me it's the balancing poses which offer the biggest challenge, many of them done standing up. I stood where I could see both the screen and my image in a mirror. As dancers do, I watched the mirror at times to help keep my body straight. I had completed more than twenty classes in this fashion before one late fall morning when my gaze wandered to the outdoors. "If thoughts do enter your mind," Riejanne would say, "just let them pass by." But surely even Riejanne would be tempted to look out the window on a day like this.

The forest was bare of leaves at that time of year and had an expansive feel to it. Spacious like the large studio on TV with its beautiful marble columns and high ceilings. My eyes drifted from screen to window. A brown cow was running between the bare trees. She looked almost joyful, as if delighting in all this space. She was moving far more enthusiastically than I was, partaking in her own particular exercise program.

Later Carl would question me about the cow. Was she alone? Which way was she headed? Did she look frightened? It seems cows do not usually run through the forest. Well I knew that of course.

For the time being, I tried once more to concentrate on the screen, on the instructor's voice. And I told myself: "If a cow does enter your mind, just let her pass by." Namaste. The breathing and stretching of yoga, writing in my journal, walking and talking with dear friends ... these practices all helped me deal with 'the confusion of another's soul' and with the confusion of my own soul. I needed all the help I could get.

Sheila vs The Hill

Journal entry December 29/04:

> Terrible tragedy in Asia with tsunamis taking hundreds of thousands of lives. We have upset the balance on earth, I'm afraid, and the climate will only become more dangerous. Is it too late to turn this around?

Turning around was what I should have done one Sunday morning when I found the bush road iced over like a skating rink. Even before that, an ice-coated car should have been enough clue to not venture out this morning. But duty called ... and a false sense of being indispensable drove me forward. How would they manage a church service without me there to play for it? I inched along the road taking a full five minutes just to reach the bend before the hill.

From January to April the procedure you follow at the bend is even more important than it is in other months. Approach the bend cautiously and as you round it, set your eyes on the hill scanning top to bottom. First, are there any cars at the top of the hill ready to come down towards you? If so, you have a long way to back up. Next, what is the condition of the hill itself? Snow-covered? Icy? Half and half?

If no one is at the top and the hill is at all icy, you need to build up as much speed as possible in the short distance, then steady it out and hope momentum will carry you up and over. Always there is a feeling of relief when you are safely at the top. "Only need to do this four dozen more times before winter is over," you whisper to yourself. In our dozen years at the lake, I had not needed to back up more than two or three times per year, and this was a good thing.

It was no secret in the neighbourhood that my ability to back up was seriously impaired, especially when curves and hills are thrown into the mix. The inevitable was bound to happen. One morning I arrived at the crest of the hill as Buster from down the road reached the middle on his way up. I knew my duty. Zigzag left. Zigzag right. Throw on the brakes to keep from going into trees. Zigzag a little more, and thank goodness! Buster was now at the top of the hill. I still had a curve or two to negotiate and we both knew how long that could take.

Buster jumped out of his vehicle and approached my car. "Would you like me to back it out to the highway for you?" "I'm so embarrassed," I admitted. Gallantly Buster said, "You know what Sheila? When I'm at work, I never back up!" It might have been reassuring to think I wasn't alone in my inability ... except I knew what Buster drove at work. He was an airline pilot.

On that icy Sunday morning the car stopped two thirds of the way up, wheels spinning. I put on the brakes but knew I was in trouble. I would have to go backwards on the icy slope. Each release of the brakes sent the car to some new angle and by the time I reached the bottom the car sat crossways blocking the narrow roadway.

Neighbours Paul and Ellen were just loading their snow-suited babies into the van when I walked up their lane. Being the house nearest the hill they are used to people coming for help. I called Carl (what did I think he could do about the problem?). Then while Ellen phoned for a tractor rescue, Paul came back with me and muscled the car to a better angle.

Carl arrived a few minutes later in the truck and immediately got stuck several yards down the road from the car. Meanwhile I looked at Paul and Ellen's two babies dressed in full winter gear, strapped into their car-seats. I thought of the effort the young couple went to in order to get them that way. Not getting to my job at the church was one thing, but keeping other residents imprisoned behind my car was quite another. I regretted my decision to put duty before safety.

Another half hour saw everyone safely back home and hunkered down for the huge twenty centimeter snowfall being predicted. It would give us lots of time to watch news reports of storm damage on the other side of the world. Our storms looked pretty small in comparison.

Fast Food

Our whole family likes to cook. Once when Michael was about eight years old he served egg drop soup to surprised guests at three in the afternoon. In addition to our family's being interested in cooking, we are likely a bit eccentric.

> Note from Michael left on our kitchen counter:
> Falafel Week!!! Preparing some chick peas for falafel, I forgot to account for water absorption. There's about five pounds of ground chickpeas in the refrigerator. I falafel about this, but what can you do?

Falafels are not my idea of fine dining. Neither is fast food, eaten in the car. But then we hadn't set out for a meal either. Coming outdoors after visiting a sick friend on a cold and windy Sunday afternoon Carl and I thought it might be a good idea to go through the drive through at the golden arches. In balmier weather, without snow banks at the roadsides, we'd have stopped at that little conservation area near the Vet clinic. But with French fries cooling fast, Carl pulled into a nearby parking lot along the Sunset Strip, and we opened the bag of food with the car parked between two rows of used Hyundais.

Carl was as surprised as I was when the little plastic mustard holder shot out from between his fingers and landed at my feet. "Can you get that?" he asked.

I looked at the items between me and the container on the car floor. "No." I said incredulously. On my lap I was balancing my purse, a container of French fries, a little bag of chicken nuggets, and one of those silly cardboard drink receptacles where the paper cup gets lodged in tightly so you have to pry it loose. Reaching my feet seemed beyond unlikely. I looked past the stack of food and belongings heaped on my knees, at the cars lined up on either side of me, price tags in their windows. So much for dining out.

Over the years we have had a lot of favourite restaurants. And lot of un-favourite ones as well. When a place is especially bad we look at one another on the way out and say: "Put that one on the list." That's the list of 'places never to go back to'. A place has to be pretty bad to go on the list, but reasons for making the (rather low) grade over the years have included the greasiest breakfast of all times, and soup which looked and tasted like dishwater.

Gilbert and Sullivan would have loved the song I wrote...

There's a restaurant I know of and I really do insist,
We put it on the list. We put it on the list.
They served us soup like dishwater
They needed to desist.
I put it on the list. I put it on the list.

Our philosophy as a family tends to be 'if we can cook it better ourselves, why go out and pay for it'. I am a reasonable cook, but I follow recipes whereas Carl cooks by instinct. This was not always the case. We had been dating a few months when Carl invited me to his apartment for a home cooked meal. The kitchen was a narrow corridor and Carl had set up a card table between the two counters so that everything was within easy reach.

I will never forget seeing Carl reach over to the hot water tap holding out a bowl of pudding mix. That sight completely blotted out from my memory, any idea of what the rest of the meal involved. Given Carl's cooking ability at that particular time, maybe it is just as well.

Are We There Yet?

In all the months since his knee replacement, we had seen no signs of progress, just pain and more pain. The Toronto surgeon dismissed Carl's complaints: "You have inflammation. Here's a prescription for an anti-inflammatory." Carl looked at his red-hot swollen knee but the surgeon was already moving on. He was seeing four follow-up patients at the same time. "Sort of like speed dating only with patients," Carl decided.

Gathering his belongings to leave, he stopped to speak to the young woman still waiting her turn: "Good luck with saving for your Accura." They had been discussing cars while waiting for the doctor to arrive. Now the surgeon approached the girl and pulled a set of car keys from his pocket: "This is what I drive." The young woman's eyes brightened: "A mustang?" "No," the surgeon replied, looking down at her, "a Ferrari."

Carl was still disgusted when he relayed the story to our family doctor. "The other two elderly patients in the room were crying, I got no help at all, and this guy is more concerned with bragging about his car than with helping any of us."

Physiotherapists were horrified at Carl's condition, expressing their concern until finally the *cavalry* was brought in and we headed to London to see Dr. R. McCalden of University Hospital. Carl expected a lot of poking and probing but was only asked to take a few steps across the room. Dr. McCalden watched with experienced eye: "You have a massive infection," he said.

Oral antibiotics could not combat this degree of infection. The whole knee joint would have to come out and a picc line would be inserted in Carl's arteries to deliver anti-biotics over the next few weeks. He would have no knee for this time, but would wear a brace as an 'external skeleton' holding the bones in place. In the cavity where the knee joint should be, pucks of anti-biotics kept the bones apart. After a few weeks, the surgeon would again open the knee and put a new replacement in. But would the infection be dead?

The day prior to Carl's surgery we met Catherine for lunch at Anna Mae's, half an hour out of our way going to London and an hour for our daughter with a squalling baby Liam in the car seat behind her. By phoning back and forth (aren't cell phones wonderful?) we were able to direct a slightly lost and very frazzled Catherine to the restaurant.

Lunch was delicious as it always is at Anna Mae's and afterwards we found a quiet corner where Catherine could nurse the baby and we could talk over our hopes and fears regarding the coming surgery. "I just want to be able to think about something other than the pain," Carl admitted. It was comforting for us to be with family as we started what threatened to be a long ordeal.

We exited the parking lot in opposite directions. Twenty-five minutes later the cell phone rang:

"I'm lost again."

"Where are you?"

"In Milverton."

"We just left there."

In truth, we had been lost ourselves. We came to the conclusion that 'all roads lead to Milverton'. It's the opposite of Walter's Falls near us at home. Once you get to Walter's Falls, small as it is, finding your way out is a challenge. Nobody knows why. But I hear that the general store there gets a good share of lost tourists trying to escape.

In the days following Carl's surgery Dr. McCalden stopped in to see him many times. His thorough followup was reassuring compared to experiences we had gone through in Toronto. In a few days Carl came home and several friends stopped by over the following week. A few days later Catherine and Stuart brought Liam up for a visit. All this company cheered Carl as he adjusted to medications and the schedules these imposed.

My adjustments included taking on the role of gardener (this damned lemon balm is not satisfied with taking over the garden. It wants the entire yard!) and chauffeur (Wednesday we take Carl back to London. I will have to manage the parking garage and if people

All Right So Far

behind me are impatient that is their problem. With Carl unable to walk I will need to drop him with Michael at the front door and just hope there will be a wheelchair nearby.)

The computer continued to be a lifeline for me. I found it calming to write letters describing the changes in our daily life.

> Letter to friends post surgery
> (knee is out, brace is on)
> May 2005:
>
> *The house will see its share of nurses in the next while. My penpal and former student, Ed from Texas, is coming to see us and Laurie, a friend from Double Vison plans to drop by. One nurse we really need to see is the home care nurse as Carl's brace appears to be slipping down and he felt sick all weekend, maybe a side-effect of the antibiotics. Today he is kind of depressed.*
>
> *Why do so few birds come to our feeders? Certainly the chipmunks have a great feed, and then last evening one of our little raccoons spent more than an hour out there. We got such a good look at her tiny pointed face and soft golden-tipped ears. Mind you she could be expensive to feed and I worry about her clawing a screen open if she gets into the habit of expecting food. I know there is no need to be feeding wild creatures as summer begins. I just like seeing them.*
>
> *I spent yesterday afternoon phoning out of touch friends to find one with bladder and prostate problems, one with a lump in her breast, and the third losing her drivers' licence because of heart and stroke problems. Makes our life look easy.*
>
> *Love and blessings,*
> *Sheila*

Our fridge was full of antibiotics which came by taxi every ten days or so. Carl was also full of antibiotics, and fed up with them by this point, with three more weeks of them to endure in order to be sure the infection was cleared up before scheduling the next surgery. He missed getting out in the world. Could we put him into the back seat of the car for an outing? The walker folded and would fit in the car trunk, but even with that support, walking was hard enough that he preferred to stay at home, walker parked in front of the stove or dining room table. Carl sat on it to prepare a birthday supper for me. He might be managing with one leg but his determination carried him forward.

I had to be determined too. Until the last few years I had never driven more than an hour from home, and only on two lane highways. We certainly do not have parking garages in any town near us. Would other drivers in the huge building be patient with me if I didn't drive fast enough? I felt so intimidated that it took two summers of visits for me to use the one in London. A few mobility problems of my own had put an end to walking any great distance.

By July Carl could sit in the front car seat to travel back for the next surgery. Dr. McCalden would remove the brace and let Carl have a knee again.

> Journal entry July 29/05:
>
> Carl is in surgery and I am hoping he has reached "the top of the mountain" and his next journey will be an easier slope. The hospital routine is more familiar by now and we both accommodate better. I find writing this journal a comfort. It gives me a focus and something familiar to do rather than simply wait, and then wait some more.
>
> 7:30 arrived at pre-op
>
> 10:00 Carl's surgery began

11:00 Picked up a salad in the 3rd floor cafeteria and have come outdoors to eat it. Hopeful sparrows look for crumbs but I have none. If I were at home I would sit in the meadow with the cicadas singing and little butterflies passing by. Here it is all concrete but at least, for now, there is sunshine.

Birdwatchers

With Carl in hospital for a while, I settled into a routine of three days in London, four at Bass Lake. Trips between the two were long but my driving skills were at least improving.

One of my favourite places to drive was the road through the Shallow Lake swamp. In spring you could pick pussy willows close to the road, although the ditches were deep enough that you had to have very long arms or not mind getting your feet wet.

A summer Saturday was the time to see large water birds. Just a year earlier I had driven this road as I headed to the village to meet my friend Jean. To the north a snowy egret stood knee deep in water only a few yards from the road, my closest sighting ever as they usually occupy the further reaches of the swamp. I slowed the car and got as good a look as I could, then continued down the road. A minute or two later I came upon a large crowd of people milling around fifteen or twenty parked cars. Birdwatchers. What else would they be doing standing by the roadside on a sunny Saturday morning. Should I tell the birdwatchers about the snowy egret, or keep him a secret to show Jean on our way back.

Jean, being a city girl, wouldn't get to see a snowy egret on the corner of Yonge and Bloor. On the other hand, the birdwatchers cared enough about birds to give up their Saturday morning. I stopped the car. "If you're interested, I just passed a snowy egret a minute or two back," I told them. I rolled up the window, and continued on my way, meeting Jean a few minutes later. I told her about the bird and the birdwatchers. "Maybe it will still be there," I explained, "but with a crowd of people like that, it has likely moved somewhere a whole lot quieter."

We approached the spot where I had seen the egret. Sure enough, a sizeable cluster of cars lined the roadside. On the south shoulder of the road, throngs of bird enthusiasts jostled one another for a position. They held binoculars up to their eyes and strained forward eagerly.

"Oh look!" exclaimed Jean, pointing over to the north side of the road where a solitary white form stood knee deep in the swamp. As far as I could tell, from where he stood, he had a pretty good view of the crowd on the other side.

Jean and I wished we had brought a camera with us that Saturday. I have been known to focus a camera on the swamp and later point out a tiny white dot in the picture. Nobody ever understands why I like those pictures.

I still had no camera as I drove along remembering the previous year in this very spot how Jean and I had laughed at the egret crowd watcher. The sun warmed my right arm and I studied the swamp beside the road. "How I would love to see some egrets," I thought. They had been noticeably absent that summer. I missed seeing them and I missed having Carl with me on this stretch of road we had so often travelled together.

I came to the first clearing where I used to see the egrets and saw in the distance a single bird. Driving a little further I leaned over and turned the radio on: *Oh my child, it will get better*, the tune danced across the airwaves, and as I reached the second clearing on the opposite side of the road I could just make out, far at the back of the swamp, seven or eight white shapes in the branches of a dead tree. *Oh my child, things will be fine ...*

Nature Calling

'THE WOODS ARE LOVELY, DARK AND DEEP'. Robert Frost could have been describing our neighbourhood, even though our forest might have been less dense than the one he described. It was a beautiful corner of the world in any case. We need to enjoy these little pieces of paradise while we still can. Because environmentally speaking, there are 'miles to go before we sleep.'

I treasure the memories of walking with neighbour Ruth through every season in the Not-So-Deep Woods: fresh green of springtime, the chatter of birds and summer hum of cicadas, dried leaves crunching beneath our feet, and crisp white days of early winter. One cold day we met an ermine who glared at us. "I have to go past him," Ruth worried, "what will I do if he comes after me?" Much as I loved animals, he looked scary to me too. I answered: "Kick him. And run."

There was a single season where Ruth and I looked at the forest only from inside. When we could not walk without fighting our way through clouds of mosquitoes we looked longingly from behind glass panes, out at the roadway winding through the trees. The lush green leaves called us, but tiny insects kept us barricaded behind closed doors.

Sometimes Nature has a way of showing us who is really in control and one autumn, beautiful as our Not-So-Deep Woods were, the whole world watched as far to the south Nature proved her point.

> September 16/05:
> It seemed to me that the local media did not handle the subject of Hurricane Katrina very effectively, but it did better than the American government. I wondered if so many resources had not been directed towards making war on other parts of the world there might have been more money left to avert the crisis in their own back yard. Predictions of calamity had been frequent enough and early enough to save lives if not property.

All Right So Far

I thought back to the only hurricane in my memory, Hurricane Hazel, which struck Southern Ontario in October of 1954. I was just a little girl but I remember standing at the living room window watching what seemed like never ending rain and hearing that people were canoeing down Fisher Street, the biggest street in our neighbourhood. This most famous hurricane in Canada's history washed out bridges and streets, left thousands homeless, and many dead.

Half a century later, we had sent a donation to victims of the Boxing Day tsunami in the South Pacific, all the while worrying that such disasters were about to increase in frequency with climate changes around the world. Even in our own area there were striking differences from those seemingly safe years of my childhood (Hazel notwithstanding) tornadoes in Ontario had become all too frequent. Our first experience with this was in the 1990's. Catherine's good friend Rebecca lived just north of us. Her parents returned home one evening to find emergency vehicles blocking the road to their home and their children.

As we watched television, we had heard a roaring sound and ran upstairs from the (safer) basement family room to look outside for the source of the noise. Despite the disturbance, a couple of miles away Rebecca and her siblings slept peacefully while a tornado ripped their garage from their house. The Ontario climate was beginning to change even then.

In our dozen years at the lake we had occasion to watch the water grow black and we knew at such a time to stay inside beyond the reach of huge hailstones. "Somebody somewhere not too far away is getting a tornado," we whispered to one another. Only a couple of years ago we felt an earth tremor from deep in Georgian Bay. And then we experienced a major ice storm.

Ice storms happen. All we can do is learn from them. Be better prepared next time. When my husband Carl and son Michael called me that February night to see the fairyland outside our sun porch, I took a few minutes to appreciate the magic. A gigantic branch had fallen across the deck surrounding the windows. I couldn't help but picture how it would look if we could place tiny lights in the fantasy world of smaller down-facing branches.

I stood transfixed at the front windows, until I realized the import of the event. If the snow was weighty enough to bring down tree-sized branches, it could easily bring down power lines. I ran to fill the bathtub with water. I looked up 'Ice Storm Survival Tips' on the internet. "I won't even read it," I called to Carl. "I'll start printing right away, just in case." The power went out after the first two pages. I would have plenty of time to read them over the next four days. The storm had things to teach us:

> You must keep a spot in the house for extra water. You can do without that bin of mismatched socks, but the water you will need.
> The freezer in winter will keep food cold three days if you don't open it. On the fourth day the top third thaws. Invite the neighbours and cook everything ... IF you have power back.
> Cooking on the woodstove goes faster if you use a lid. Obvious right? Some of us learn slowly.
> Don't use the sink for dishes as the water cools too fast. Transfer a large pot back and forth from wood stove to sink and reheat as needed. (Thanks to Carl, country-raised, for showing me that trick.)
> Every day an hour before dusk gather your candles and matches in one place. Do supper preparations early but don't eat too soon. Guaranteed, the evening will be long enough.
> Now, as evening falls, is the time to remember childhood word games like 'Ghost' and 'The Dictionary Game'. In the dim light 'I Spy' could be a challenge ...
> Take your camera outdoors to capture the magic and the destruction.

Well into the fourth day we heard a helicopter flying very low. Michael and I watched from the bedroom window as a figure clearing out the mailboxes at the road disappeared in a flurry. Above his head, the chopper created quite a storm blowing snow off the power lines and we were relieved to be safe indoors rather than caught in the resulting whiteout.

While the ice storm imprisoned us spring seemed far away, but within weeks the long winter finally ended. Patches of snow still dotted the forever changed landscape, and residents and cottagers alike surveyed the ravages left in the wake of the great ice storm of 2006. Many trees stretched sideways or arched bizarrely across the roads. Giant branches hung, snapped from strong trunks, pointing unnaturally downwards but still bravely producing leaves ... for a time. The evergreens looked most hurt, snapped off at the tops with jagged trunks aimed skyward. Over the next two years branches closest to the top would reach up in increasingly vertical lines as if taking over for a fallen comrade.

It seemed so long ago that I sat with my family around the wood stove wearing three layers of sweaters and at the coldest times, a fur hat. But in a few weeks winter gave way. We cleared away the large branch and an entire tree, which had also fallen across the front deck, and with their removal the raccoons lost their playground.

As the woodlands came alive again we could look out our window at the masked figure perched on the edge of the half barrel planter, little hind paws dancing my new Martha Washington geranium into nothingness, our baby grandson pointing from the door "noon! noon!" So often I fed the "noon" when he stood at the bench outside my window with his three sisters, thin winter-starved bodies and noses covered endearingly in bird seed.

The creature turns liquid brown eyes towards the door. He does not understand about my Martha Washington. He just thinks a new feast has been laid out for him in the white wire bird feeder located, as I realize too late, conveniently close to the planter and just high enough for two furry hind legs to stand and reach it. He has lost his winter gauntness. Summer is around the next corner. The sound of the chainsaw is heard in the land and woodpiles are high once again. We will outlast the mosquitoes or scare them away with liberal slatherings of Avon *Skin-so-Soft*. There will be walking in these woods again.

Comfort Objects

Long before there was light I woke. This was the morning of my cataract surgery, and though I had been assured it would not hurt, I felt nervous. I reached down to stroke the purring heap near my feet. Abby yawned and stretched as my index finger sought out the familiar spot beneath her ear. Half of my mind watched her blink encouragingly at me while the other half remembered my phone conversation with Catherine the previous evening. "Liam hasn't chosen a comfort object," she had explained. "We offer him that cuddly white lamb you gave him, and he likes it, but he's not especially attached."

Catherine's own comfort object twenty-eight years ago was a pink teddy bear who grew increasingly shabby. We washed, and then at certain stages where we could no longer coax the flattened fur into a measure of respectability, replaced him, but Catherine was not fooled: "Mommy bring teddy in a bag?" she inquired suspiciously, sniffing the fatter, fluffier substitute teddy. Carl and I called each successive model "teddy" despite a one-time proclamation from the small owner: "I think I'll call my teddy ... Linda."

At ages two and four, both our children received homemade koala bears from a family friend. Years later, Michael's "Joey" was still around, faded to a dull brown and worn with love. We operated on him when Michael was about four years old. Gave him a nose-job complete with bandages. Catherine's koala never needed surgery, be it nose-job or tummy tuck. A couple of dozen years later, "Joey's" twin still looked like new, or at least not like 'old', due to less overall handling and hugging. The koala was ever present, but the comfort object remained ... Linda.

Left arm extended, I felt for the furry body of Abby, stretched out against my back. This dark morning, as I tried to think of anything other than today's surgery, stroking the warm fur soothed me. When I switched the lamp on, I noticed beside the bed, a battered felt mouse with half its stuffing gone. Abby had brought me the gift of her own comfort object. Little as I might value a battered felt mouse, I appreciated the gesture. Smiling in the dark I came to a small decision: "I think I'll call my mouse ... Linda."

How does it happen that you go from a "no cats allowed on furniture" position to sharing your bed with one? I think it started with little Nick who, when he came home from the vet's with just weeks to live, assumed, rightly, that we would deny him nothing. He stretched his silky black form across the previously forbidden bed and seemed to smile at us.

Once you have allowed a cat, any cat, on your bed, you are definitely on the downward slide. All future cats will automatically be granted the same privilege. And every cat finds the thickest comforter or the softest blanket to curl up on. You look at the cat, snuggled on the folded quilt, and actually struggle with your conscience: "I might need that blanket spread out over my legs later in the night, but she looks so peaceful there. I hate to move her and take the quilt away."

Decades of married life passed before we bought our first ever duvet. It was feather light and soft just as we expected but the intricacies of duvet care were a mystery to us. "Every few days you get on one side and Dad gets on the other," Catherine explained, "and shake it hard to redistribute the feathers." Forgetting to do this resulted in clumps of feathers in some parts and a cover with no stuffing in others.

Next we learned about washing the duvet. This knowledge resulted from the unfortunate encounter between the duvet and a piece of blueberry pie. I had heard on the radio that you should put a tennis ball in the dryer with the duvet. The radio gave no instruction in getting the cover back on the duvet, but the best results seemed to result from reaching not just arms but heads and shoulders inside the covering. Eventually I developed a technique of standing on the bed for extra height, holding corners of duvet and cover together and letting everything fall to the floor.

Beneath the duvet I sometimes use an electric heating pad down at foot level to take the chill off before climbing into bed at night. A couple of generations ago warming pans were the way to go, although that was only for the rich. I pity the pioneers with a fireplace growing cold overnight and a mattress made of straw.

Our own mattress was too rigid so we covered it with a sponge pad called an egg-crate to make it more comfortable. I bought an especially thick one and it worked great until the time came to wash it. The only method I thought of was to spread the egg-crate on the deck and take a hose to it. Drying such a thick layer of sponge brought its own challenges. It had to be done on a sunny summer day. Once the pad was soaped and rinsed thoroughly I squeezed what water I could from it. Then I dragged it into the sunniest spot available and every half hour or so turned it in different directions or moved it to the newest sunny spot.

It was the difficulty in laundering that inspired me to buy a thinner egg-crate. What? Give up on the comfort? Not a chance! I put the thin egg-crate on top of the thick egg-crate hoping only to wash the thinner one. What I didn't plan on was the combined thickness of mattress plus two egg-crates, and how to pull a fitted sheet over the whole thickness.

Changing the sheets had to be done in secret in our house as the cat was fixated on clean sheets. When we took in Abby as a five week old kitten, she was so tiny I brought her into the bed for comfort on cold evenings before she went to her own bed in the sun porch. And in time she developed this *thing* about freshly changed sheets. She often stood guard as I changed the bedding and there were times I had to make the bed in steps: bottom sheet, remove cat, top sheet, remove cat, quilt, remove ... "There's a bump in the bed," Carl warned whenever I came back from loading the washing machine. And sure enough, if I bent over and listened to the bump, it was purring.

Emergency

A FEW MONTHS OF 'NORMAL' HAD LULLED US into a false sense of security. Battling our way back to the marriage we had lost for a while, had not been easy. Carl did what he could out in the world to remain useful. I played my music, wrote my stories, baked my cookies, and once again knew the joy of being married to my best friend.

Carl had defeated an e-coli infection and had his knee replaced twice. The initial surgery had resulted in an infection running rampant through his system. The brain condition once diagnosed seemed to be forgotten by the medical people, as if to say: 'There, we gave you a name for it. What more would you expect us to do?" We had finally begun to understand that there was nothing they *could* do.

We knew the previous summer's infection was still in Carl's body. We did not know it was gaining control. It seemed each summer's health journey was wilder than the year before. Our normal life was about to be switched for one where ambulances hurtled through the forest, followed by taxis delivering medications, and nurses bustling in and out of our home.

That Friday morning in mid-July I kept hearing a sound like Carl clearing his throat. But I knew Carl was not at home. He had left for town about 8:30. Still, I checked the house twice, looking in every room to see if he had come back. As I reached the sitting room door I glanced outside. Carl lay on his stomach in the driveway. The scene from *On Golden Pond* flashed through my mind, wife cradling dying husband. I rushed outside. Carl could barely raise his head.

Running back in for the phone I dialed our nearest friends and neighbours to come. Carl insisted I should not call 9-1-1 and blindly I complied. I could not get past the feeling of removing my husband's right to make his own decisions, even with him face down in front of me on the ground. The Grahams who lived seven minutes north of us arrived. David looked at Carl lying motionless in the gravel. "Call 9-1-1," he said. I needed that permission to push aside Carl's wishes and take the necessary action.

The ambulance attendants loaded Carl into the vehicle and I climbed into the front. As we pulled out, Dave Greig arrived at the outer gate and I could only look at him sorrowfully through the window and wave as if we were part of some ghastly parade. Six hours at the hospital failed to turn up the cause of Carl's collapse. With the brain disorder being so rare and unheard of, doctors could only wonder if it could have caused this collapse. Later I would think we should have Cathy diagnose the problem: "It has to be the infection back," she had insisted.

Thankful to be back home, we headed to our front deck and watched a family of baby blue jays learning to fly in the bright summer sun. Such excitement, their little cries a higher pitched version of their parents' shrill voices. Despite the hot temperatures Carl dragged a thick comforter out onto the deck. He could not warm up. After a while he returned to the couch where I hovered over him talking on the phone with his sister Helen, both of us anxious. Once again Carl told me not to call 9-1-1 but his skin was grey ... "ashen" the ambulance attendant called it twenty minutes later.

This time I took the cell phone, my emergency bag, my contact list, and my own vehicle to get home later. Neither of us had eaten all day but Carl wanted only liquids. I brought him bottle after bottle of his favourite strawberry-kiwi drink from the vending machines in the hospital lobby.

With a mother's instinct Grandma Katie had sensed that something was wrong. She called relatives to drive her to the house but of course we were not there. Once home she called my mother, so that both Grandmas who we had not informed in our efforts to shelter them from the day's pandemonium, were now very concerned.

Cathy had reached Michael at his blacksmithing course in Haliburton. He should not try to come home til the following day, she told him. A greater concern was how and even whether, to inform daughter Catherine, dealing with a precarious second pregnancy. Did we dare tell her? Did we dare not tell her? She would be upset either way.

While Carl struggled in Owen Sound hospital those two days, Catherine threatened pre-term labour, trying to stay off her feet with ninety-three days til the due date.

As I explained to the policeman who stopped me for driving too fast up by the hospital, I was plagued by the thought, and the reality, of having loved ones in two different cities both needing me. The officer shook his head. "You have enough on your plate without a ticket," he said. "Have a good day."

Although Carl's conversation made sense at the time, he would remember almost nothing of these few days. His body systems were wildly out of control. The old infection had regained its footing, and then some. His knee, scarred from three surgeries already, grew hot and swollen. He was in septic shock.

Leaving the hospital around nine on Saturday night I drove home and crawled into bed. But tired as I was, my uneasiness prevented me from sleeping, so that despite having been with Carl just an hour earlier, I put the lights back on and dialed the nursing unit.

"We're sending him to London by ambulance first thing in the morning," the night nurse announced. "He'll leave about seven or eight ... as soon as they can get it together."

My mind was fully alert now. I could drive to London but I would need a place to stay. On/off ... On/off went the computer ... it was dial-up all the way, out in the Not-So-Deep Woods. I searched for a Bed and Breakfast, made phone calls, wrote e-mails, all while trying to throw together a suitcase of necessities. What would Carl need? Leaving a phone message at the B&B I turned the Internet back on to send a backup message. In case they didn't check their phone maybe they would pick up their e-mail.

This was before the days of Facebook where people are informed at a moment's notice. But there on my screen, from Jacqueline, my young writer friend: "If you should need to go to London ..." Jacqueline could drive and her mother Orrene would offer a place to stay.

More phone messages. More e-mails. More packing. I set an alarm for six a.m. Needn't have bothered. I managed three hours sleep and woke to the quiet dark. Even the birds would not be up for another hour but I was anxious to have time with Carl before he left. Michael had come in from Haliburton the previous night. We reached the hospital by five-thirty, but no ambulance had appeared by seven ... or by eight.

Around nine Jacqueline arrived. We learned that although Carl needed surgery in London and was manifesting a number of scary conditions, there would be no ambulance to take him.

"You'll have to take him by car," they said. My patience was nearing its end.

"This man has fallen through the cracks of the system at every possible juncture," I told the nurse who seemed to be in charge. "If it weren't for medical mistakes he wouldn't even be sick like this. And now he is being let down again."

"There's nothing we can do."

Every ounce of assertiveness in me rose to the surface. "You'll be reading about this in my next book."

The nurse laughed.

"I have two published already." The nurse wheeled around and left the room. Michael followed and returned a few minutes later. "They're calling for a helicopter," he said.

Carl travelled by air, a trip he would normally have found exciting. But he was much too sick to notice much beyond the ceiling of the chopper. Helen drove the roads from Tobermory, reaching Carl's hospital room about an hour behind Jacqueline and me.

Jacqueline had gone ahead to Carl's room. She inclined her head slightly and widened her eyes as I entered. "I am your daughter-in-law," she whispered. Only close relatives could spend time in Carl's room with his being so ill.

With a gentle courtesy unlike his normal boisterous self, Carl asked repeatedly for water. Staff explained kindly that in case the surgery could be done that same day, he could not have anything by mouth, even a sip of water. He had spent all day and much of the night before without a drink and the summer heat made this condition even harder. A sympathetic nurse rushed in with a fan to at least help cool him. I wonder if that nurse ever knew how much her small kindness had meant? Carl talked about the fan for days afterwards.

We expected Carl out of surgery in a couple of hours but did not see him until nine that night. Over the next day and a half an assortment of nurses, doctors, respiratory technicians, lab staff, and physios paraded through Carl's room, singly and in bunches.

Carl struggled to breathe. Again and again people asked: "Do you have COPD?" This stood for Cardio-Pulmonary Disease. The heart and lung specialist explained to Carl that having been a smoker for much of his early life had caused chronic bronchitis. Added to that, sleep apnea was aggravating the atrial fibrillation. Carl needed a CPAP machine but I knew the chance of his consenting to that was minimal.

Being a patient in a teaching hospital meant a constant stream of medical students and their instructors passed through the room. "Do not trust the readings of machines measuring pulse rate," one doctor advised the group standing at Carl's bedside. "If the reading says one-forty it is more likely around one-seventy." Carl's monitor read a hundred and fifty. I drove the three hours back home, the doctor's warning lingering in my thoughts.

Hospital

The suddenness with which Carl developed serious heart and lung complications following his lifesaving surgery felt bewildering to both of us. Like those scary times of the last two summers, the machines registered very high pulses, and to make matters worse, Carl struggled to get air.

"There is a flopping sensation in my chest," he complained.

"This comes from atrial fibrillation," the heart and lung doctor explained.

"Your sleep apnea is aggravating the condition."

Doctors waited and watched for heart and lungs to normalize. Hospital had become Carl's world, and connecting it to his old life felt important to me. I took in two beautiful photos of Liam to sit by Carl's bedside. I knew the blue eyed rosy cheeked child in the pictures would provide a conversation piece and a way for staff to enter their patient's pre-hospital world. I kept one foot in this world and the other at home, thankful that I had enough driving ability to make the trip to and from London.

Once on my way out from visiting Carl I noticed cars pull quickly to the curb in front of the hospital as a security guard ran towards them. These drivers knew the drill. Most likely they were hospital employees and had seen this happen before. Faces peered over the cement walls of the parking garage and a mixed crowd of patients in wheelchairs, visitors carrying shoulder bags, and staff with name tags flapping in the breeze, trained their eyes on the helicopter rising straight up between concrete buildings. How Carl would have loved this sight. But he lay upstairs on the ninth floor.

Days later Carl still could not walk, but his bladder which had not worked after surgery seemed to be improving, and his pulse was thankfully normal after all the uproar when it ran at high speed. One night Carl's PICC line came out. How glad I was that this didn't happen at home where it would have meant calling a nurse in the middle of the night. I could imagine the nurse driving out through the forest, climbing from her car to unlock the gate, looking over her shoulder for bears.

I went home for a few days and spent a happy afternoon looking at old photos with my mother. It was thirty degrees even in forest, so Mom's second floor apartment would have been dreadfully hot. What a relief not to be in London in this heat.

Catherine had now completed twenty-nine weeks of her second pregnancy and had stopped dilating at three centimeters. Hopefully she would continue to hold steady despite experiencing a lot of contractions and back aches which felt to her like labour. Her physician and her midwife disagreed about the amount of danger and nothing could be done except wait it out. Our niece Erin was born at this very stage twenty some years earlier and she turned out great, so I celebrated the milestone by buying a two piece pink velvet coat and pants set with matching hat, all covered in tiny rosebuds. We were ninety percent sure the baby was to be a girl. I did not even think about a little boy dressed in all those rosebuds.

They brought Carl north to Lion's Head in early August but our joy was short lived. An angry red swelling appeared on his second day there. "He has no fever," they told us. And the "bump" becoming redder and angrier looking, was a hopeful sign as the infection might be coming out the top instead of going in deep. Either way they expected to take Carl back to London as soon as they received word from the surgeon there. This could mean another ride on the *knee-out-knee-in* roller coaster.

If surgeries number five (remove the infected joint) and six (insert yet another one) might be waiting just around the corner then we would make the most of having the civic holiday weekend together. Michael and I loaded Carl into a wheelchair and headed down to the beach where people were building sand sculptures. Wheelchairs do not roll in sand but we got close enough for a good look at a very large mountain lion sculpture stretched out along the beach. That night there were fireworks by the water and the staff offered to take patients to a window where they could see the display, but Carl's mind had moved two steps ahead to London and he felt too discouraged to join in the celebrations.

Carl's fifth knee surgery in three years, and his second in a month left him less sick than previously. His heart weathered the storm this time. The infection was a new one. As bad as this might sound, it was the best possible news under the circumstances. The knee replacement was not infected ... only the incision site above the knee. We would watch closely from now on viewing with suspicion every occasion of pain, heat or swelling. The original infection might live in his body all the time, necessitating the taking of antibiotics all his life. But that would be a lot better than losing his leg. Inwardly I cried, "Just let him walk while the brain condition still allows that." The timing of this infection seemed so cruel.

When I left for home, Carl was just able to get to a sitting position at the edge of the bed. Within days he could walk to the door of his room. Then he pulled a muscle trying to do strengthening exercises, so that was a small setback. Our greatest hope was for him to return to Lion's Head soon. Forty-five minutes to the little village hospital would be a pleasure to drive compared with three and a half hours to University Hospital.

Time was right for the "bump-out effect" as I call it (one thing gets better and another gets worse.) Catherine was ordered on bed rest. How do you do that with a toddler? Through this challenging pregnancy, Stuart had taken all the time off he could without jeopardizing his job. I went down to Guelph to help as much as I was able.

Letter from Lynn Wyvill:

Sheila,

My heart goes to you today. You are carrying a large load, with a lot of stuff out of your control. Be brave girl, and trust the strength is within you, when you least expect it. I know all that stuff you are likely hearing about how God never gives one more than we can handle, but there have been times when I felt the dear Creator got me mixed up with someone else. So let your friends carry some of the 'stuff'. And be happy in this time with Carl. As painful as it must be, it is really a time just for the two of you. God bless you.

Love,
Lynn

Aug. 18, 2006

Hi Lynn,
I will take you up on your offer to share our sadness. Thanks for that.
The good news: Carl is back in Lion's head as of last night. The bad news: the infection may live in his body forever.
People ask why on earth we are not suing the original surgeon who in his arrogance insisted there was no infection, and caused three subsequent years of suffering. But our basic belief is that what you fight makes you weaker. Can I guarantee we will hold that position through another three years of this unhappy dance? Maybe not, but as it says in that funny poem about the optimist falling ten stories: **All right so far.**

Love and blessings,
Sheila

Happy Anniversary

During that summer which Carl spent in hospital, we had reached a milestone anniversary. It was particularly important to us since we had worked so hard that year to save our crumbling relationship.

As the date approached, I thought about the party we held for my in-laws' 35th anniversary so long ago. The farmhouse was alive with friends and neighbours enjoying cake and ice cream, congratulating Katie and Stewart on a long marriage. And now, we had reached our own 35th anniversary, one without cake and ice cream, one without friends and neighbours. At least Carl had been transferred to Lions' Head hospital, blessedly closer than London. I searched the china cabinet for the special knife we use for family weddings. Engraved on the blade: Carl and Sheila August 21, 1971, Stewart and Katie June 14, 1941, Jack and Helen October 13, 1973. Tucking the knife, a cake, and our wedding album into the car, I headed north.

Celebrating your anniversary in a hospital room would not be anyone's choice but at least this room had a big window which provided a pretty view of trees across the street and a source of fresh air. Helen arrived with a vase of flowers and fancy napkins. She and Jack live about thirty-five minutes north of Lion's Head. We cut the cake, shared it with whatever hospital staff we could find, and reminisced about our wedding day.

In the album we all look so young. I am sitting in the wicker rocker at the farm, gold locket around my neck, bouquet held by arms so slim I can hardly believe they are mine. There in the group pictures Carl looks handsome. Best man Dave has not changed all that much, but look at my brother Jody. He was just sixteen in nineteen seventy-one. The dresses my mother and Katie are wearing bring me back to the moment I came out of the farmhouse in my wedding dress. They exclaimed in excitement about my dress, and I was equally excited about how everyone else looked. Katie's dress was teal blue and she wore a pink corsage. Mom was dressed in pale yellow with dainty black shoes.

My mother looked so young in that picture. A widow, still raising a child, she had limited financial resources. But she bought the flowers for our wedding. I look at the bouquets and the corsages in the photo and see how pretty they are and feel grateful for such a generous gift. I would not be throwing my bouquet, tradition or no tradition. This was a custom I disliked intensely. I did not intend to see as a part of our special day, a bunch of elegantly dressed young women scrabbling over some flowers like a pack of dogs after a bone. The bouquet went to my grandmother back in a North Bay nursing home.

Another tradition I was determined to avoid was the clinking of cutlery on glasses to have the bridal couple kiss. Once would be okay. After that I would like to enjoy my dinner thank you. Carl and I shared a kiss and then in my typical camp counselor style I explained to the guests that they had just seen the only kiss. Anyone clinking a glass from now on would have his fork taken away.

Carl's relatives did not know me very well. Within two minutes a guest applied fork to water glass. Carl helped me out of my chair, and held my train aside. In a flash the offending fork was confiscated and we finished our meal with no further interruptions. I look back now and hope I didn't spoil their fun. I can imagine them looking across the tables at one another: "Well, that's a school teacher for you."

Some anniversaries we give gifts to each other. Other years we don't. There are no rules about this. It just feels right certain years, and this thirty-fifth year I gave Carl a little clock mounted on a case that held photos. Family photos, especially ones of little Liam, had been pretty important this summer when Carl had not been able to see his grandson.

I had not expected that my husband would have a gift for me. How could he possibly buy one in a hospital. So one day in London, when I noticed an inexpensive but pretty watch in the gift shop downstairs, I had bought it and taken it up to his room. "I hope this is okay with you," I began. "We can put it away and it will be your gift to me on the twenty-first." Carl had agreed that this plan was fine and that the watch was pretty. What he did not tell me was that he had already arranged his own gift.

Now, from amidst the bedding and clutter of meal tray, magazines, telephone and medical equipment, Carl pulled out a tiny box. "I asked Michael to make this for you," he said. Nestled in the box was a pendant, Michael's trademark leaf design in shebuichi, a pink coloured Japanese metal, and set against that, a petite silver lily. "The back of the leaf is rough," Carl explained, "to represent our last few years, and the front is smooth for a smooth road ahead." Oh, how I hoped he was right.

Date Night, Medical Style

We got Carl home the last week of August. He had 'missed' an entire summer. As much as anyone wants their longtime patient/loved one to come home, chaos erupts while the spouse/care giver races between hospitals and pharmacies picking up medications and supplies. When the patient's home is in the woods, those hospitals and pharmacies take time to get to, and in our case were located in opposite directions. Whether heading to Owen Sound or Wiarton I could thankfully check on a Grandma and pick up groceries while in town. But leaving Carl unsupervised for long made me anxious and I rushed to do the *have-to's*.

On Carl's second night at home he loaded his pump with antibiotics and almost immediately lost colour and became dizzy. "It feels as if someone is jerking my neck back," he exclaimed. The home care nurse I phoned told us to call 9-1-1 immediately. Another ambulance came charging through the woods. This time we went to Wiarton hospital. In the hushed emergency ward the doctor shook his head. No explanation for the strange reaction could be found. But Carl seemed normal enough now. He could come home for the night. Calmer now, we drove the back roads in the moonlight with quiet music playing on CBC's night programs. To my addled mind it felt like a date.

Life resumed some sense of normalcy. But through the PICC line in his body, Carl continued to administer his own meds three times each day, a complicated process.

> Journal entry August 28/06:
> Thankfully Carl can usually see what needs to be done to fix the pump for his meds. But sometimes his weak wrists and my arthritic fingers prevent us from closing the pump.

So *normal* was a relative term. At times the nurses were unable to reach a doctor to prescribe Carl's heparin. For two hours or more Carl would struggle to get the meds to go through the line or flush the tubes after whatever amount did go through. Because the next step of leaving messages for nurses and waiting for them to get back to us started late every night, only a few hours remained for sleeping. Then we would need to get up early for the nurses to come out and try to get control of the situation. I was exhausted. Carl was frustrated and irritable, threatening to pull the lines out of his arm and saying he would have to go and live in a nursing home.

Letter to Catherine September/06:

Hi Honey,

The nurse called to say they don't have any prepared needles so they left a package in our mailbox. Your Dad is filling the needles. He and Michael both understand how to do this stuff. As for me, I copy down the written instructions but am fairly bewildered by it all. Our friend Liz who used to work as a nurse told us that patients now do what nursing students were not allowed to in their first year only a short time ago.

Catherine's pregnancy was still holding. She was partly dilated with the baby in position so travel by car was out of the question for her. But after two months without seeing her or Stuart or Liam, Carl was desperate to get there, so Michael and I loaded him into the back seat of the car in a prone position, the biggest pillow we could find stuffed in behind his back.

A few days later I looked out the window in the early morning to see brother-in-law Jack perched on a tractor, followed by a huge gravel truck. He and Michael worked for many hours that day to raise the driveway so that Carl would have only a single step to go up from driveway to veranda.

Letter to Jack September/06:

Dear Jack,

I remember a Christmas in those years when we had too little money and you had too little time, I watched you talk to your girls about the gifts Carl had made for them. Was it the Victorian cushions or the stained glass lamps? I remember how you spoke straight from the heart, about how this was more than a material gift, this was the gift of their uncle's time and thought, as he fashioned each little gift with his nieces in mind.

Since Thursday, we remain astonished at your own gift of time, thought, and energy. Your vision for how it could be, and the hours of hard work you and Michael put in that day, will make day to day life easier in this third challenging summer. It will ease some of the physical pain Carl experiences trying to get from car to house. No small thing, for him, or for me as I watch him struggle.

For so many weeks our life has revolved around hospitals and the highways that lead to them. Bringing Carl home to our little corner of the woods Tuesday brought its own comfort, but I have become too used to watching for ambulances through my corner window. Looking out and instead seeing you chugging along through the forest on your tractor, leading the huge gravel truck, felt to me like the cavalry is coming.

Love and Blessings
Sheila

The Not-So-Deep Woods represented our personal shelter and sanctuary. But not the easiest place for medical people to reach. After a while, nervous as we were, we did not call an ambulance anymore. Carl seemed weakened in every respect and decades older. I recalled hearing older people talk about having *spells* and it seemed to me this was a good name for the reactions Carl had to some medications. But we had become hardened to the sight of a nurse struggling to get the PICC line to accept meds. Nurses worried that trying to force the injections through could have serious consequences but luckily that did not happen. Carl had been using all his strength to push the needles. Probably it was a good thing that his strength right now was limited.

London was not just a city to us now. We used its name interchangeably with the word hospital as in: "London says to bring a bag with him tomorrow in case they need to keep him there." "London will have the IV team sort out why his PICC line is still acting up." Carl had a heavy weight hanging over his head. Soon Dr. McCalden would check the knee again. Please, not another surgery.

I kept Catherine, Helen, and Ruth informed with e-mails:

> *The nursing team now have a plan for changing pumps when he comes back from London but they will not order new equipment til they know he has seen the IV team, so we have at least thirty-six more hours of struggling at home with the current setup which does not work.*
>
> *The medical supplies which we needed today have not arrived but a card came in the mail to say a package will be at Wiarton Post Office at 5 pm, so I will head over, hoping it contains the supplies we need.*
>
> *Our life lately is like being on a merry-go-round we never asked to be on, and the only blessing is that it occasionally slows down so friends can wave at us. You three are my inner circle. Bless you for being there. Keep waving.*

'Normal' is a Relative Term

I usually looked forward to the magic weather of mid-September, but this year I was distracted by a sore and painful mouth. It was hard to tell whether I had two separate conditions (tongue damaged by jagged tooth where a large chunk broke off, plus sore throat preceding a cold) or if the tooth was infected and was spreading contagion through the tongue and down to my throat.

The only bright side was that this might be a way to lose weight since I could eat only mushy stuff and even that, very slowly. It took a half hour for a 'meal' (bowl of various kinds of mush, biscuit soaked in milk worked best. I longed for toast but mainly ate nooketli (noodles Carl made by hand) for suppers and porridge for breakfast. More and more frequently I broke into a sweat, waves of fever washing over me. The dentist's office had told me I must wait several days to get in. In the end I waited a hundred hours, counting as they went by: "Only sixty more hours to go."

I thought it best to surround myself with light in as many forms as possible. I got outside on sunny days. In the evenings I lit candles to brighten the house. And I counted on friends to add a brightness of their own.

Our friend Jean, the violinist, had been through some serious health issues of her own but we hoped to get together soon. She wrote that in order to go into classrooms to share her musical gifts, she would be required to submit to being checked out by the police.

Letter to Jean W. September 21/06:

Hello Jean,

The thought of you needing a criminal records check in order to play music tells me how paranoid our society has become. You certainly look dangerous. Maybe there is a machine gun in your violin case?

Carl was relieved not to have to stay in London yesterday. They put chemicals through his IV line but still have no explanation for the dreadful reactions he has been experiencing. Doctor McCalden is allowing three more weeks before a final decision regarding another round of knee-out-knee-in *surgeries.*

Love,
Sheila

Carl could manage getting in and out of the car and navigate steps better than before, but being invited anywhere to visit meant lugging along all the medical paraphernalia. Still, it would be worth it, we thought, when invited to Jacqueline's in Meaford for conversation and a taste of her wonderful gingerbread cookies. Barely an hour into the visit Carl's IV lines and pump went berserk. *Beep-beep-beep.* This was a familiar experience for us, but having it happen in someone else's home was nerve-wracking. *Beep-beep-beep.* The alarm made conversation impossible. *Beep-beep-beep.*

We sat in Jacqueline's living room, Carl increasingly frustrated and trying his best to re-set the pump's computer, but the insistent noise continued for a full half-hour. Apologizing all the way, we retreated to the Meaford hospital only to find staff there afraid to adjust a computer, which was not theirs.

A frantic ride in the car followed, with the computer beeping all the way. Thankfully every twenty-five seconds we could press a button to silence it but there are a lot of twenty-five second intervals between Meaford and Moo Alley. Our nerves were on edge by the time we reached Owen Sound, and doubly so when we finally arrived home and a nurse came out to sort through the problem.

Nurses knew where to find us by now. It was common to find a computer message on Carl's pump warning: *air in the line*. Whenever we saw the line dotted with many bubbles we shut the machine off and waited for medical help. Carl had to call again on Thanksgiving weekend. Trying to lift a heavy roasting pan with turkey onto the stove, he sliced the IV line in two by catching it in the oven door. The nurse who came to his rescue bent over with laughter: "Only you, Carl! Only you could do this."

Focused as we were on our own health concerns, we had plenty of loved ones with their own medical issues. Stress levels played havoc with Michael's sugar levels but thankfully our own family doctor, even though he was a forty-five minute drive away, had agreed to add Michael to his patient list. My mother struggled with bursitis but her health until now had been good and she was amazingly independent for her age. Unfortunately she had been unable to find a doctor in Owen Sound, which like so many areas of the province, had thousands of 'orphan patients' needing care.

After a summers' worth of 'baby threats' only three weeks remained in Catherine's pregnancy. We would feel truly blessed if this new little one could just be as happy and healthy as Liam. Now at almost twenty-two months he put words together and sang little songs, trying to do actions. He noticed everything around him. When Catherine took him through the MacDonald's drive-through one day she heard a little voice from the back seat giving 'his order' ... "Two chippies (French fries) and two toys."

Luckily there were days when we put aside everyone's health concerns and invited friends. Sometimes we did potluck. Other times we picked up pizza or Chinese food to share. It was a little cold by the time it got that far from town, but nobody cared.

In the verandah garden we had grown miniature hollyhocks, about three feet high in my favourite shade of pale pink. How often I had looked at those flowers over the summer, wishing Carl could see them. And now, since the flowers had lasted into the fall, he could. A nice distraction from needles, pumps and nurses.

Alarm

Thousands of blackbirds had flown through the Not-So-Deep Woods in those Indian summer days. I always looked forward to seeing and hearing them once each fall, but this time flocks of birds came three days in a row with the forest singing for fifteen to twenty minutes each time. About a hundred would go over, with a few seconds pause, and then we would see another hundred, and another. The first day I timed the length of the fly-by to a good twenty minutes.

While I rushed out on the deck to watch the birds, Carl sat on the couch. Getting up was just too hard. Increasingly he saw himself only as "the patient." I didn't feel like care giver, but neither did I feel like anyone I had been before. My role as wife had changed dramatically. Little of the writer-me had survived though it still lived somewhere deep inside. My musician self lacked spirit, feeling more like an observer than a participant. This was not fair to the church. I knew it, and the church board must have known it as well.

Finally I reached the decision to leave my position. I spoke to a couple of key people and sat down to write my letter of resignation. It felt a little like giving up, but most of all brought a sense of relief. I could no longer do the job the way I had once done, the way I still wanted it to be done. I doubt my departure took anyone by surprise. "Thank you for the consideration you have given me during our family's health challenges of the past few years and in particular, this difficult summer," I wrote. The church had been more than patient with the roller-coaster existence we had ridden in the past half year.

There were times when my body may have been on the organ bench, but my mind was more with Carl. Following a leave of absence over the challenging summer I had gone back and done the necessaries but when I looked up in the loft and Carl was not there anymore, I lost heart for being choir director, the part of the job I had always enjoyed most. Over the years, at the larger church and now at Shallow Lake, Carl and I had developed a way of bantering back and forth at practices. The close-knit choir missed Carl's musical ability, but his teasing manner left an even bigger hole.

Where a group of us used to enjoy going for lunch after a service I now rushed out the door in my hurry to get home to Carl. Some Sundays we got the Grandmas out to the lake for lunch. But both were frail and struggled increasingly with their health. Visits involved driving in figure eights to pick them up and take them home afterwards as one lived to the north and the other to the south.

If I left the church job, I could concentrate more on family. By the time I played my last service at Shallow Lake, the forest was empty of birds.

Panini Generation

Late in the afternoon I usually walked in the woods. I weighed my priorities. Husband. Grandmas. Children. Carl and I had our feet planted firmly in the *sandwich* generation involving ourselves in the lives of our children and our parents. My brother Bob once said, "Not just a sandwich. More like a Panini generation."

Our new grand-daughter came into the world on her great grandfather's birthday. I set out at dawn knowing Catherine had begun labour the night before. Stuart's Mom Freide lived closer if support was needed in a hurry and was probably there already. My role was to stay a few days to help with cooking and little ones.

Over the summer Catherine and I had often discussed this day. "Stay in hospital for two or three days," I had advised my daughter. "Rest a bit before you come home." Catherine used what we call in our family the Sellwood philosophy. Milt Sellwood, a vice principal in our early years of teaching used to advise us to, "smile nicely and do it your own way." I should have realized my determined and independent daughter would follow this course even having laboured all night long, and given birth a few hours earlier.

At noon, Catherine appeared in the doorway, baby carrier in hand. Instead of two or three days she had barely stayed in hospital more than two or three hours. As a gift from the baby, she and Stuart entered the house lugging along some rather large toy trucks for Liam. They hoped this would help him feel kindly towards this new little being who would now share their attention. Liam could already identify several colours, count to fifteen, say the alphabet, and sing several songs. Often we heard him sing "Tinkle tinkle yiddle sar ...". But he was still a baby himself, several weeks short of his second birthday.

On the other *slice of the sandwich* Grandma Katie appeared physically ready for a nursing home but loved people and bravely got out and about whenever invited. Excursions could be a bit scary for those of us accompanying her. She seemed so frail and shaky that we often feared she would fall. My mother, Thelma lived in a tidy little apartment handy to the city buses she liked taking downtown.

We recognized that not many people our age have the privilege of including parents in their lives. It was good that we lived just a half hour from each of our mothers. At the same time, in my heart I longed to live nearer to the kids. Carl and I talked about moving an hour further south. Years ago Carl had taught me to examine decisions by asking: "How would it really be?" We had moved before ... three times. There was the stress and work to consider, but even more we asked ourselves if we were ready to leave the place we had dreamed of living in for so long. Our decade at the lake had been happy and we had expected to stay there for another ten years. Still, we were driving to Guelph weekly, spending more time getting there and back than actually being there with our family.

Emotionally I went through a tug of war: kids ... lake ... kids ... lake. I felt as if I was part of a scene from Camelot, my spirit singing *If Ever I Would Leave You* (It couldn't be in spring time, autumn, winter, etc.) Each season has such beauty on our little cliff above the lake, and well we knew, there would not be a property like this in an area we could afford. We wondered about the Markdale area. Could we center our daily life there but still keep in regular contact with our closest friends from around Wiarton?

Letter to friends early December 06:

> *Gwyneth is a gorgeous baby and like her brother before her is easily calmed by the stove fan. Why do babies all like that roaring sound? We bought Liam the movie Polar Express and he is fascinated by it, sitting through the whole thing without moving. We celebrated his second birthday a week ago. Already he uses lots of little sentences and makes us laugh with phrases like "Holy cow!"*

Both Grandmas are increasingly frail. Katie needs much help and the lion's share of helping is done by Carl's sister Helen. My Mom battles bursitis and is having surgery for skin cancer in two weeks. They have rushed forward with this procedure as she refused treatment for so long and there is now some urgency. Her walking is much worse and I worry she will fall. She knows that now she must hang on to railings to protect herself.

We are still thinking about moving. Clearly, Carl's health requires us to be in a very accessible house. The infection must be watched closely but there is an 'early warning system' of fevers and increased pain to indicate if it is getting out of control so hopefully we can keep him from ever becoming as sick as he did this past summer.

Love,
Sheila

My mother's facial surgery in December left me admiring her courage but worried at how fragile she had become. Her incision resembled an upside down flowerpot covering one whole side of her face and extending down into her neck. It was frightening to see this, let alone be changing dressings on it, but the bleeding settled down around midnight and she did not need much help during the night. Within a couple of days she was able to change her own dressings. Brave little Mom, I thought.

Carl fretted over next steps for his leg. If the infection remained out of control the options facing him included doing the surgery over, fusing the leg, or even amputating.

"All this worry is crazy," I scolded. "Phone down to London and see what our next steps are."

Never had we been happier to hear about a medical mistake. It seems that when the doctor last read the results from Carl's blood tests, he somehow went back a page and read a previous result. The office nurse checked her records: "The numbers are actually down," she assured him. This gave us the most hope we had known in three years. Despite balance and mobility issues, just not having to face more operations would mean so much.

Christmas Eve Katie called to say she thought Mom was in difficulty, Carl and I hurried into Owen Sound to check her incision which she thought was redder and more swollen than it had been. Carl's walking being difficult, he waited in the car while I ran in to the apartment building. The scar looked no different to me than it had looked a day earlier and I convinced her to wait it out. We drove back home, stuffed Christmas stockings and crawled into bed.

At 11:30 Michael woke me, "Mom, the package of prescriptions we picked up from the drug store is missing the insulin and I am right out." Frantic calls to hospitals left us unable to get the right kind of insulin, but he headed out to get a shot of any kind and the welcome news that a drugstore would open in twelve hours.

All this was happening on the heels of Michael's losing his job the Friday before. He and Sara had just put a down payment on an apartment in Brampton and they planned to go ahead and move in despite the job loss. Michael would keep looking for work. His eye surgery a week and a half earlier had gone well but we felt some concern. He has been diabetic since age four.

Thankfully Michael found an employment agency which hooked him up with a job. The work was not very pleasant but it would pay minimum wage to look after bills for a while. At least he had all the same shift, 4:00 to 12:30, a necessity for keeping good diabetic control. Everyone hoped that his little nineteen eighty-something car would hang on, as otherwise he would be left with no way to get to and from work. Struggles aside, everyone knew Michael was a good person, honest and reliable. You just had to watch his gentle approach with his little nephew, or engage him in conversation to see the kindness shining through.

Real estate-wise, we had made no firm decisions but tried to clear out clutter as if we were moving. Living a bit further south would put us further away from the Grandmas, Carl's friend Dave, and sister Helen. I would also be removed from my dear friends Ruth and Cathy, but living nearer to our children was a big incentive as was the possibility of locating minutes from a hospital and other services we might need. I had a good talk with Elizabeth McKinlay who had once lived in Markdale and now lived in our old house at the North Acre. She said, "Sheila, you just don't have enough information yet." She was right. It felt like "yes, but not yet."

The floor plan at Moo Alley was open and easy to navigate. But if anything went wrong mechanically, a low crawlspace with dirt floor complicated the problem. One winter night something seemed to be leaking and we needed to know what it was. I could not believe that Carl with his physical limitations managed to make his way beneath the house. Crawling being out of the question, or at least I had thought it was out of the question, with the much beleaguered knee, I suggested he try to go in on his back. It was no use my going as I wouldn't know where to go or what to look for.

This situation pointed us once more in the direction of moving to a home with better accessibility. Once Carl emerged from under the house, I breathed a sigh of relief that he at least made it under and back out. Stains on his pant legs showed that he had tried to crawl on his knees. I didn't even want to think about that.

This particular winter had us all feeling as if we were "crawling on wounded knees." Michael with his financial struggles, and Carl and I pushing forward along the sandwich generation road a few inches at a time.

Appearances

Appearances don't matter. I want to believe that. But there are times (like in real estate dealings) when suddenly they do matter.

Moving or not, it made sense to upgrade the bathroom and move some upper cupboards to open up the kitchen to the rest of the living area. The house would look a lot better as soon as we got past the first rule of renovations: before it looks better, it has to look a lot worse. We knew that of course. We just didn't trust anyone visiting us to know it too.

For years we had teased Catherine about her response as a teenager anytime a family member reported taking a tumble on the icy street. "Did anybody see you?" she would ask. Something seems to happen to kids between the ages of thirteen and fifteen to make standing out in any way in public extremely distasteful. I imagine my younger mother self arriving home in casts and braces. My daughter is at the door looking very worried: "Did anybody see you?" she asks.

Certainly there are times I prefer not to be seen. For example, there are those rainy days where my hair, even if freshly washed, turns to a frizz reminiscent of Bozo the clown on the popcorn boxes we used to get at the movie theater as children. And as for my house, well here is a riddle to consider ... When do you want the aunt and uncle you have not seen for two years to visit? That's the aunt who, kind though she is, looks like she stepped off the cover of Vogue magazine, and whose house, at least in your imagination, is always in perfect order. When will they arrive?

Answers: a) when you are cleaning your laundry closet to get room to put some of the clutter caused by the renovations; b) when every single surface is covered in a thick layer of drywall dust; c) when every item from the bathroom is sitting out in the family room; d) when you have a housekeeper hired to help you clean up the mess the next day; and e) all of the above.

> Journal Entry (when you can't cope anyway, you might as well write in your journal):
> Have dragged stuff all into the sun porch and swept up as much of the dust and dirt as I can sweep. Am comforting myself with (editor) Anne's words: "I hope things go smoothly but if things don't go smoothly I hope you at least get a story out of it." I think I feel a story coming on. My aunt and uncle are on their way out. Lets see if they recognize me through the dust.

After all my anxious dithering, the visit is short but pleasant, with the tidiness of the house and state of renovations not discussed and maybe not even noticed. We wave goodbye to our company and I enjoy a bath before settling down with a book. Within minutes, the phone rings. Our kids are in the throes of selling the first house they have ever owned and have warned us to be available at this hour in case they need advice.

In no time flat, I will be worrying about appearances once again. I will barely have time to pick up the phone before it goes dead and I need to make a giant mental Note to Self: *Do not forget about the* "who's going to see you?" *issue.*

"Don't take time to put clothes on. Just throw your coat over your nightgown." When my husband says these words, distant alarms sound in my mind. The proposal is all too familiar. The last time Carl said these words, I ended up in a strange man's kitchen explaining why I was dressed this way. The last time he said these words, his broken down car was nowhere to be found, I almost ran out of gas, and I had to back down (and backing down any kind of distance has never been among my driving skills) the stranger's long driveway in an outfit never meant to be seen beyond my own doors.

Although the house phone has mysteriously died, we do have a cell phone. What we don't have out in the Not-So-Deep Woods is reception. I look down at the long flannel nightgown. My inner voice cautions: "At least take time to put on your pants." I hang up the dead phone, picturing my daughter on the other end. She is wringing her hands in worry: "Why did Mom say hello and then hang up? She knows we called for important advice. She wouldn't just hang up like that. Has something terrible happened?"

I face my husband who is heading for his jacket in the closet. "It will only take a moment to dress," I tell him. But Carl is adamant: "Oh for heavens sake, we're just driving down a country road to some place where the cell phone will work. Who's going to see you?"

"Who's going to see you? Who's going to see you?" the words echo in my mind. That's what he said last time. But sometimes we ignore the inner prompt, the whisper we know should be listened to.

It may be hours before the phone works again. In another city our daughter waits for our advice on the sale of their house. She probably has the papers in her hand. She's feeling pressured to sign. She needs us.

Carl jingles the keys. "Who's going to see you?" My wiser self loses the battle. The dutiful wife, who ought to know exactly where nightgowned excursions led by her husband can take her, nevertheless dons white fur-topped mukluks, throws a heavy coat over her long white nightgown, and steps out into the snowy night.

Postscript:

Thank you very much John and Helen Harrison for welcoming us into your home, letting us use your phone, and above all not thinking it at all strange that I had come visiting in nightgown and snow boots.

Three Minute Mission

WE COULD HARDLY BELIEVE A SPRING AND SUMMER had come and gone and it was autumn again. No ambulances. No hospitalizations. Carl fought pain every day. Walking was a challenge. But he had resumed a fairly normal life. "If I'd known you wouldn't be sick this summer, I'd have arranged a holiday," I told him. But living on a cliff overlooking a lake, every day of your life is as much a holiday as anyone ought to want.

We drove down to the Grey Highlands area a couple of times that fall scouting out properties. Should we move or not? I trusted we would be led where we needed to go. Surely I was being led in my search for Carl's birthday gift. Carl had no idea what we were looking for. But in that month or two before Christmas, from years of shopping experiences, he drove the car without asking too many questions. He was a good chauffeur, experienced in being the husband of a musician-writer who tends to be a magnet for peculiar circumstances. Besides being a musician-writer I was a good navigator ... usually.

That morning it had seemed possible that we could run an errand on the other end of a long day. That morning it had seemed possible to locate a music store in a strange city. Now with the early winter sun hanging low in the sky, and my energy level even lower than the sun, I considered how to go on a hunt for my husband's birthday gift. "Wait 'til tomorrow," counseled a lazy voice inside my head. "Carl's birthday is still three days away." A more responsible part of my mind uttered a warning: "Tomorrow you will be back home with few resources. Right now you have access to city stores." A music store was what I needed. Being in a city offered an opportunity I must not pass up.

McGregor was a street our son-in-law had mentioned might have music stores. But I had no map, and only a couple of landmarks to identify the neighbourhood. Anyone could find landmark number one, the beautiful church, its spires pointing into the sky. And almost immediately we drove under the railroad bridge, my second point of reference, but I did not see McGregor anywhere. Tiredness got the better of me. I would look for five or six minutes only, I decided. "I don't know where to go," Carl said. His voice sounded a bit peevish. He was tired too, and he did not even know what the errand was. "You'll have to give me directions."

Directions? I didn't have a clue. From the fog of weariness I heard my voice instruct: "Turn right." Turn right? Why did I say that? I had no idea where I was going. Carl wheeled the car around the corner. What was I doing? I couldn't keep giving directions to a place I didn't know by a route I couldn't begin to imagine. My voice continued: "Take the first parking spot you see." With the car stopped I might get my bearings. The first parking spot turned out to be the only open parking spot in the entire block. I climbed out of the car and looked to my right.

A music store. It looked dim inside and bare, and not in any way promising, but I went in anyway. The owner wore dreadlocks. In front of him on a stool sat an old woman who looked even more rundown than the store. They both seemed surprised to see a customer. "I play keyboard," I explained, "and my husband could use some brushes to play along, but I see you don't sell instruments." Actually it was hard to tell just what the store did sell, and I wasn't sure I wanted to know.

"Just a minute," said the man walking a few steps to grab a rectangular black case. "I'm a drummer. This is my own kit," he said as he opened the case. "You see I have two sets of brushes here. They're not perfect but I only need one so I can sell you one set for fifteen dollars."

Now I don't have any idea what a set of brushes should cost, but I wasn't going to look a gift horse (or the Universe who sent me to it) in the mouth. I pulled a five and a ten dollar bill from my wallet. Clutching my purchase I returned to my startled husband. I had been gone from the car a total of three minutes. I had my brushes. I had my story. What more could a musician-writer want?

Have I Got the House For You!

My neighbour Ruth and I kept in regular touch every winter when she went to Zambia to work as a missionary. Ruth loves *warm* and in that way I think Africa was good for her in winter time. But I wondered how she coped with living at such a great distance from friends and family. Sometimes she walked a mile to a place where she could access the Internet only to find on arrival that there was no electricity right then.

So those times when she pined for home, and I looked around my forest half a world away, feeling too secluded, especially if there was a full moon we thought of each other. I had told her of a song sung by Miriam Makeba, known as 'Mama Africa', called *Same Moon*: *Same moon in sky over me, Same moon I see her eyes see*. I thought of Ruth as I looked out my window through the bare snowy branches.

Though few visitors found their way to the woods in winter, one afternoon Jacqueline came for a visit. Mid-afternoon Carl left for a meeting and had gone as far as Owen Sound when he called back: "I'm not going any further, and don't let Jacqueline leave," he warned. "It's very icy and the visibility is poor too."

Since he had already reached the edge of town he picked up pizza to bring home. Outside the storm raged on but inside it felt like a party. For Jacqueline it was a sleep over. "Couch cushions on the floor are fine," she insisted. Right. I could imagine Jacqueline waking up often in the coming night, cushions shifting to leave gaps and spaces. The next house we live in will have a guest room I promised myself.

Jacqueline's company cheered us hugely. Visitors had become few and maybe that was part of the reason moving had begun to appeal more I can only blame the loneliness of winter for inspiring us to drive further south and look at houses we would not ordinarily find attractive. I think cabin fever is a real condition, and I think we had a bad case of it.

Surely some kind of fever possessed us to consider the property on the highway. The spacious house had a good layout ... and that's about all. It sat close to the neighbour's yard which sheltered a number of old dead cars, and if we could have seen beneath the *snow garage* I expect we would have learned it came with its own dead car too.

From letters to a friend:

> *Stage 1: We put in an offer on the house in Markdale and then found out there is a municipal landfill 2 km away. So we are investigating as we have to know the land, water, and air are safe. We need to see environmental reports, do inspections, talk to engineers. Perhaps I am to learn about patience through this. I don't feel very patient, for sure. It will be disappointing if we have to back away, but for now, one step at a time.*
>
> *Stage 2: The house inspection is tomorrow afternoon. Following much thought and discussion almost to the point where it is a 'discernment process' we feel reasonably at peace with whatever happens. We see potential due to the size of this place but if there are structural problems we will let it go. Brother-in-law Jack is going with us and the important thing will be to take his professional advice.*
>
> *Stage 3: Our real estate offer did not go ahead so we are watching again and even wondering if we have the courage to build one more time. With Carl unable to do any of the work now, it would be a much different process from what we ever knew.*

My letter, while telling what happened, could never be described as telling 'the whole truth and nothing but the truth'. It would have taken a lengthy letter to fully describe the house inspection on the real estate disaster we nearly bought.

The house inspection team had already begun working when we pulled up to the house. Our agent Mike arrived about the same time. Brother-in-law Jack was pacing back and forth in front of the building. "It was built in four parts," he told us. Carl might have known that did not bode well. I was blissfully ignorant of the complications which might arise from building a house piece by piece and stacking those pieces together like a Lego creation.

We spent a half hour roaming through the house in various combinations: Carl and Mike together, Jack and I together, the three men in a group and me alone, Carl and Jack huddled in a corner talking while I happily described possible upgrades to Mike. The house inspectors were cheerfully doing their job, but we could have saved the fee as Jack's building experience more than qualified him to assess a house. Finally, one of the men suggested we adjourn to a nearby restaurant for coffee. "Coffee," he called it, but we all knew the real reason was to carry out a review of what we had learned ... more of a postmortem as it turned out.

Mike drove to the coffee shop in his own car granting Jack a few crucial minutes with Carl and me. Jack, the most effective salesman I have ever known, used the few minutes of travel time to acquaint us with the fact that the house had huge problems. In the restaurant he skillfully guided the conversation in a way that prepared us for letting the house go.

From loose railings to insulation problems, from rusting on the roof to a nightmarish electrical system, from dangerous woodstove and chimney to mould on bedroom windows ... the house would need much time and money to fix properly. When Jack finally got us alone in a second restaurant later that day he leaned forward and spoke straight from the heart: "Please don't buy this house."

It was good that I had such a grand map of Southwestern Ontario. Each time I came home from visiting Catherine over the next few months, I checked different side roads for houses which might be for sale. At home I looked on the Multiple Listing Service so often that I knew which houses our agent Mike was likely to tell us about next. We had asked Mike to keep us within ten minutes of Markdale. We needed a change of lifestyle and it had been a very long time since we had lived within ten minutes of anywhere.

From Markdale we could still reach friends north of us but have a shorter commute to see our grandbabies. The decision had been long in the making but now we hoped only to get on with the process.

Going to look at properties distracted us from being lonely, and also from health issues. Then Carl's face began swelling. Some days it swelled more, and some days not as much, but it was enough to make us uneasy.

Letter to Jean:

We are still trying to get Carl into an endocrinologist as three doctors have recommended since early January, but the local doctor says the specialist is just too busy. Carl's face swells often and his legs balloon up constantly. My nurse penpal Ed wonders if he may need his lymphatic system drained.

The other evening a mother and baby porcupine crossed the road in front of us. The baby was very little, half the size of 'our own' porcupine at home, and it could run. We would rather not have 'our own' porcupine of course. Porcupines love to chew things and it remodeled our bird feeder into a more open air design. There are also the raccoon diners who stand at the little bench at the end of each winter and nibble on birdseed. We hope that whoever might buy our house will be an animal lover.

Well, that's the news from Moo Alley where we are fresh out of raccoons and porcupines but still see the occasional rose-breasted grosbeak at the feeder and hear a loon calling on the lake.

Take care of yourself.
Love and Blessings from both of us,
Sheila

Packing it Up

I HAD LEARNED A NEW CONCEPT through the winter just past, when Elizabeth McKinlay told me, "You're just going through the process of discernment." As the winter passed I had been increasingly aware of what we would be leaving. With the sun streaming in from the east I often looked out at the lake below stretched under its snow blanket. The white surface brought back memories of those years when Carl and I took snow machines out on the farm to play hide and seek through his Dad's farm acreage.

Carl always had the advantage. He was strong. Certainly strong enough to lift the snowmobile backwards if he inadvertently ended up with the skis straddling a tree. Which of course he never did. And which of course I did more than once. Carl's second advantage was that he cheated. If he could not find me, he would shut the engine off and listen. That made it easy for him to *win* since winning involved following the other person on the trail until he (Hah! More like *she*!) turned around to find her opponent smiling broadly and triumphantly ten yards or so behind her.

If, with the engine shut off, Carl did not hear the sound of my machine, he headed for the forested part of the land knowing I would more than likely be found sitting, one ski on each side of a tree trunk waiting for rescue. His cheating mattered far less than my being rescued so it all worked out. The area we explored was not big enough to get lost in, but a walk back in deep snow to the farmhouse would have been cold and tiring.

A lifetime later in our own woods, it was time to admit that we had spent our last winter at Moo Alley. We moved on into spring, contemplating our future. One day we drove south through the Grey Highlands area. Carl turned the car off the main road for a better look at the pond we were passing. As we came around the corner I spotted a tidy little brick house with a for sale sign in front of it.

"It's probably beyond our budget," I told myself, but we stopped and chatted with a woman in the driveway for a few minutes, getting a feel for the location and the view. I could hardly wait to get home to the computer to see the listing, holding my breath 'til I knew it was in our price range. We were on the phone to Mike in a flash, and set to see the house the next day.

My mind flew as we entered the house. Hardwood floors, big windows, two baths and laundry all on the main floor. It didn't have the open concept we were used to, but otherwise everything we needed was there including forest behind and pond in front.

I wished the old Carl, the strong of body Carl, could be back to help me prepare for the move. I started packing books and photo albums first, sliding the heavy cartons along the hardwood floor into Michael's room. Through his young adult life Michael lived in our home and out of it in turns, depending on what work he could find and how far he had to travel. He came home and packed up what remained of his belongings which blessedly needed only a quarter of his room to store. Daily I dragged and pushed and pulled more cartons into his room, onto the new floor. When Michael had lived in this room the floor had been covered by a too old, too ugly carpet, but as people so often do, we fixed up the place for whoever would live there next.

I did a lot of the packing at night. I was up anyway worrying about how I would ever get it done, so it made sense to me to use the time. I turned on the electric fireplace in the sitting room, and in nightgown and padded slippers, stacked boxes higher and higher.

Twice Ruth came and wrapped dishes with me. I zipped my trusty electric scissors across a heavy roll of brown paper spread across the dining room table, and Ruth lay plate after plate on the sheets for wrapping. Somewhere we had found out that plates should be packed on their sides to lessen the chance of damage. We enjoyed our visits as we worked and Ruth who knows me so well asked many leading questions concerning the preparations. I am not a sequential thinker and am likely to miss important steps. "Have you thought about how you'll be transporting the cats? Will there be a place to put them at the new house while the movers are going in and out?"

Another day Jaqueline showed up with the gift of her youth and strength. She could work three times as fast as I could and in a few hours my entire collection of books disappeared into boxes. I looked around gratefully at the cartons filling Michael's room and half of the sitting room. I couldn't believe how much had been accomplished, but if I stood beside a stack of boxes it reached higher than eye level.

I compiled lists of furniture and drew optimistic floor plans showing how fifteen hundred square feet of furniture was going to fit into twelve hundred square feet. I worried that Michael was lifting far more than doctors wanted him to do with his back problems. Also, I was straining my arthritic fingers, and Carl was feeling demoralized over what he used to and could no longer, do.

Dear friend Cathy knows us so well. What would she think of our decision to put the house up for sale? As always Cathy looked for the positive, reminding us, "You two need to start believing in yourselves again." A wake-up shower of truth from a friend who has always understood us, and told us with love what we needed to hear. A gentle form of tough love, and I am grateful to her for this observation.

Cathy offers apologies for her admittedly terrible typing. But she writes in a flow of consciousness style more from her heart than her head.

Her words are beautiful and they ring true:

> *A way on to the future for the two of you, closer to your kids and your babies, out of the wood and into the meadow so to speak. That little shady Moo Alley was a great place to nest and recuperate and now out you go into the world and make a haven for yourselves to nurture your family and entertain your friends and read uninterruptedly and listen to music and watch the sunset and make it all serene right after the hammering and banging and updating of bathrooms and dismantling of walls and replacing of windows. I think whatever you do, you will do what is heart, and what is heart is energizing and what is energizing is good. Nothing is written in stone or dust, or drywall for that matter. There will always be options.*

Cathy was right. Options were what we needed in our increasingly lonely neck of the woods.

Katie's Purse

THE SANDWICH GENERATION STUFF never lets up for long. But the bottom line is, it is a privilege to be part of the lives of your parents and your children.

Throughout that school year Catherine and Stuart's neighbourhood had become *party headquarters* as university students moved into house after house nearby. They were torn between loving their little place and knowing it was just a matter of time 'til no other families remained on their block. Better to move on, move forward. Move.

The middle of flu season had not been an ideal time to go through a whirlwind of packing up babies in snowsuits so the house could be shown. All Carl and I could do was murmur our sympathies over the phone hearing how our young family went from leaving the house a couple of times a day, to eventually saying, "Sorry, it's just too hard. We'll stay out of the way, but we have to be here." Suddenly their house was sold, unsold, and re-sold within a few days and only five weeks remained before the move.

Catherine described how she looked down while signing papers for the sale and realized there was a pen in one hand but she was wearing a sock puppet on the other.

About this time Michael had another setback. His X-rays were bad: degenerative arthritis of the spine. No longer allowed to bend and lift, this development meant he must stop working in the warehouse where he was currently employed. He had diabetes, eye damage, and attention deficit disorder. "Why would we hire you?" was the attitude at interviews. Michael never asked for help and we worried about him running out of food or insulin.

At the other end of the sandwich generation, both Grandmas were struggling with health issues. Grandma Katie, had become very ill in March, going from a reasonable degree of independence to needing total care. We stood around the surgeon as he explained his findings: a baseball sized tumour in her bladder had metastasized to her lungs. Despite her frail condition they had operated to try to take away the discomfort as much as they could. Words like *very aggressive* and *palliative care* left no doubt concerning the seriousness of the situation.

Michael came home to see Katie and a few days later, on Catherine's birthday, she and Stuart brought the babies too. Liam added much joy into an otherwise challenging day singing a lot of songs for us, some parts very in tune, many with all the words. He and his Dad had made what he called a "happy cake" for Catherine. We brought my mother out for the birthday lunch and she enjoyed the family time but was sad about Katie too. Michael had been attending job interviews but with no encouraging results. His last diagnosis put him in a tailspin for a while as he could not think how he could work if he was no longer allowed to lift and bend.

'Life and death' were never far from my thoughts. I had in my mind the wise words of a dying friend: "No, it's not a sad time," he had said, "I am seeing everybody." When he told me that, I thought about the word 'seeing' and realized it also had deeper meaning, like when we really 'see' with our hearts into who another person is.

For a long time when the phone rang I still thought it was Katie. She called often during those last years when she couldn't walk as easily. She loved being with people and walked to see them as long as she could, and then the telephone became her next best connection. So the phone would ring or we would be going over to Wiarton for groceries and I'd catch myself thinking, *we could call Katie and take her out for lunch*. And I'd have to remind myself that we couldn't do that any more.

We brought Katie's purse home those last few days of her life. She was getting sicker each day and she wanted it looked after. At first, we left it in the sitting room waiting for her to get better. Only we knew she wasn't getting better. In a week or so I moved it first to the bedroom, then to the closet. Retiring the purse to an out-of-sight-out-of-mind location felt like an admission of failure: "There's nothing you can do."

The day came when we gathered around Katie's bed. "Did the nurses call you all to come?" the doctor asked us later. And no, they didn't call us. We just saw Katie getting weaker and more tired, and once that evening she roused enough to ask who was there. She knew her children and her beloved nieces were with her. She had seen every grandchild that last week and a half. And she had told friends "I won't be going into the Home." And so she didn't. She chose her time, and we gathered around her bed and Jack said a prayer of thanks for her life, and I sang *Stay With Us Through the Night*, and Katie avoided going into the Home.

I couldn't look into the black leather handbag for many days. But then Helen needed her mother's social insurance number and her health card. I had to look ... inside the closet and inside the purse. Looking into another woman's purse feels like an unpardonable intrusion. Even with my own purse, my husband always asked permission if he needed to get some change out. I didn't want to look in Katie's purse. I returned the bag to the closet floor until we had to pay a bill with Katie's money.

Opening the tiny bag inside I removed three twenty dollar bills. I put them in a big white envelope and labeled it: "From Katie's purse." When I only needed one of the bills, I wrote an accounting on the front of the envelope. No one was holding me accountable. Least of all, Katie.

I picture Katie in the back seat of our car, opening that little black bag and pulling out a ten dollar bill. "Gas costs money," she would scold, "you take this." We would throw the bill back and forth at one another until finally Carl would have the last word: "Mom, you cut this out or I won't take you anywhere anymore." He had the last *word* it's true. Often he did not have the last action though, as we would almost always find the ten dollar bill hidden somewhere in the car.

We talked as a family about the contents of Katie's purse. Maybe we could make a donation from the little wallet to some great organization like Habitat for Humanity, or Doctors Without Borders. Then we got thinking of a Christmas gathering months away and remembering how Katie got more excited about Christmas than anyone we ever knew. We could wait 'til Christmas and use the money to buy a turkey and other treats.

One of the granddaughters would make Katie's plum pudding recipe, and maybe another would bring her fudge to pass around after dinner, just as Katie did so many times. And as Katie did every year, we'd get out the little Santa she always loved so much, which all the rest of us hated, and we'd let it roar around the house playing the worst Christmas music imaginable. Everyone would laugh as we watched Katie's great grandbabies chase the offending Santa around the room. And we'd smile at each other and say, "Wouldn't Katie have loved this?"

Essential Services and Peaceful Places

Despite having prepared Moo Alley to sell, we seemed to be on hold. People came to see it and were usually effusive in their praise for our corner of paradise, but we had to wait it out. Nobody could complain about spending summer listening to loons in the morning, and watching the sun set through the trees.

In the meadow lay a fallen log with an indentation just my size and shape. The sun warmed this open field for hours after it had disappeared from our forest, and I always enjoyed watching the little rust-coloured moths cling to the clover. Here the crickets sang and I felt contentment like nowhere else. It became increasingly hard for Carl to walk up to this spot I called my peaceful place, but in an uncharacteristically romantic comment he once told me, "*You* are my peaceful place."

As summer slipped by I realized how little time I had spent down at the lake. I made a promise to myself: "If it's four o'clock and I am still working at the computer, I will shut it off and go to the dock." For two days I kept my word. On the third day, I thought "just a little more work," and as if provoked by my broken promise, the computer shut down in mid-sentence. Soon, though, we discovered we were not alone. Most of eastern North America was also without power.

The heavy demands of people seeking cooler spaces in this hot week were too much for the system. Individuals and businesses alike tried to conserve energy once the power was restored. Catherine, working in a government office, stayed home at first, and was sent home when she tried to go in on the third day. The guard at the door asked, "Are you an essential service?" The 'essential services' at Moo Alley were food (safe in the freezer if we kept the lid closed), lighting (lots of lanterns, candles, and flashlights), and toilets (water for flushing drawn from the little wading pool, too cold to swim in and finally useful in this unforeseen way).

A week later, in a violent thunderstorm we again lost our electricity. But there was no peaceful shutdown this time. Instead came a blast of thunder so loud that my feet left the floor. A tree collapsed across the lines on the main road left us in the dark for about twelve hours. But the road was a fifteen minute walk from our door. How could the blast have sounded so close? We discovered the answer a day or so later. Just in front of the house a ten to twelve foot strip of bark and wood had been peeled from one side of a tree.

I had always thought lightning hit the highest point. But the stricken tree was not particularly tall. I thought of those people in Kelowna BC where the summer's lightning had ignited several huge forest fires and ousted thousands from their homes. Life brings no guarantees. I could not know if my peaceful place would stay peaceful. I did know by now that lightning could strike our quiet forest, and that illness and discord could reach into the hard-won peace of our marriage. If you know that storms may come you can keep an eye out for them. You can hold one another as they pass by, knowing that on the other side of the storm, there is peace again.

Those twin trains of health and marriage crisis I used to imagine? One was going downhill to be sure, but slower than it might have gone. Carl and I stood side by side at the controls of the second train. We understood now that we were driving. Storms or no storms, we planned to stay on the tracks.

Letter to Carl

LETTER TO CARL:

"The days are long but the years are short." I have no idea who said that. But it is so true, my love. Some of those days we spent in hospital and some we spent fighting ... how those days dragged. And yet I can reach back to that time we stopped being you and me and became, as you once told me "just us".

I always knew who you were. Perhaps better than I knew who I was:
In earlier years you drove the boats and flew the kites,
Sang your songs and danced your dances.
You combed the ditches for flowers
You cooked up feasts for friends,
A hammer in one hand, a paintbrush in the other.

Calendar

Winter - the beginning

January 1970
    You had been so ill over Christmas that you almost died. So ill that the doctor made house calls. I didn't know any of this of course. I went with you to the Dairy Queen once, but you were just a guy I worked with.

February 1970
    When the children asked about our first real date, not counting the Dairy Queen, I had to confess that we went to the Groundhog Dance. Anyone from outside Wiarton Willie Country will do a double take at that, but where you grew up the prediction of spring is serious business and the Groundhog Dance was a highlight of early winter. I still have the little groundhog pin which was a combination admission ticket and souvenir but I don't really need any souvenirs of that evening to keep it in memory. I remember how soft your cheek felt as we danced together and how your mother made pancakes in the farm kitchen after the dance.

March 1970
    The road was snow packed and dark beyond anything I had ever experienced. "Just stop for a minute and listen," you suggested. We stood still and for the first time in my life I knew the total lack of sound.
    For a few weeks now you had been bringing me out to the country, to get to know your family "That's the girl Carl is going to marry," Helen had told your mother.
    How different the place was from the small city where I had grown up. So I stood, with the man I would indeed marry, just listening to the silence.

Spring - courtship

April 1970

The farmhouse was full of tiny bedrooms and your mother gave me my own little apartment those times I stayed over. There were always rag rugs on the floor and flannelette sheets on the bed, and there were probably mice but I didn't know it. Katie hummed as we did the dishes, and you chased her with a vaccuum cleaner and threatened to pick her up and put her in the sink. It was a totally different way of treating mothers than I had ever known. Was this what they did in the country?

May 1970

Just as your mother had laughed when she found me digging up stones and moving them out of a flower bed ("stones are what our earth is made of here" she told me), you were amazed that I was counting the trilliums. They told us in school we must not pick them and I thought they were rare. I got to two hundred before I gave up.

June 1970

"This place is special to me," you explained, indicating the point of land where we stood, and the lake around us. It was good that you loved water, because I loved it too. Crickets sang and maybe frogs, though I don't remember them . . . but it was spring so why wouldn't they?

We went back to the farmhouse, and the livingroom I had assessed as being so full of personality: yours, as it turned out . . . tree branches indoors couldn't have been your mother's idea.

We had to keep the music quiet. Your parents were already asleep upstairs, but you put on a record (no CD's in those days) and we danced. "You are my special angel," the singers confessed, and you stopped dancing long enough to kiss me ... for the first time ever. The big armchair had room for two. I felt so cherished.

All Right So Far

Summer - long days, short years

July 1978
>We come back from a swim down at the shore to a big pot of spaghetti and a pan of homefries. This is what we used to do when we were first married. Only now we are leading one child by the hand and carrying the other wrapped in a towel. I look at you and think "Aren't we lucky?"

August 1985
>The lady at the Bed and Breakfast calls up the stairs: "So sorry to disturb you but your mother is on the phone." A rare time together without kids and invariably one of them gets sick. At work the next week, a colleague of Carl's shakes her head in disbelief. "How can you spend money on a B&B anyway," she asks. "It's an investment in our marriage," he tells her.

Autumn - hurricane season

September 1999
>"Your husband has an e-coli infection...

October 2001
>... a brain disorder ...

November 2002:
>... a life-threatening condition."

And it's winter again. Already. Wasn't it just a little while ago we stood on that snowy road and listened to the silence, our life as a couple stretched out ahead of us, invisible, beckoning.

December 2002
> Choirs, concerts, carol sings. I so strongly believe that when groups of people sing together a special spirit connects them. Maybe that goes for couples too. Carl and I spent a lot of years singing together. We can't dance much anymore. There has been too much physical damage. But we can express our love to one another. We can receive one another's love.

So far, despite all the challenges, or maybe sometimes because of them, we can still be in the world together, creating. We hold one another, supporting and supported, and inside us the song plays:

> *I never knew it would be like this how could you bring me here?*
> *But once again Life whispers in our ear:*
> *They're still playing our song.*
> *Just listen to the music.*
> *That's all we need to do.*

Epilogue

"Sheila, I'm sorry," my friend Joan said, as we drove north along highway 10. "But somebody has to tell you this. You understand, don't you, that this book ends when Carl dies?" My response was to go home, and over the next week, bring the story to a close, mentally dusting off my hands in a 'that takes care of THAT' gesture.

I knew Joan was right of course. And Carl knew it too. We might not know at that time what his condition was called, but the reality was a steady loss of the abilities we all take for granted: can't walk unsupported, can't walk at all, can't stand.

This story was not over.

It would be many months before we understood that I could end Part One now, while we really were, in the words of the title, all right, but in time there must be a Part Two to the story, one which must ultimately offer a sense of hope and humour. Working on it, Friends. Working on it.

About the Author

Sheila came to Grey Bruce as a young teacher, married and raised two kids and a series of cats. She directed choirs in several area churches and played keyboard in dining lounges. Always she wrote, but aside from newspaper and magazine articles, did not begin publishing until 2003 when the Brucedale Press put out *Somebody Move the Cat!* her book of light, often humourous personal essays. Sheila followed this with a similar collection called *Our Side of the Fence* in 2005. The inspirational memoir All Right So Far, has been a long time coming but is the book she and husband Carl wanted out there, hoping other couples would identify. Set in the woods above beautiful Bass Lake, not far from Georgian Bay, it tells the story of how health and marriage issues nearly ran them off the rails, and paints a picture of two ordinary people at a not so ordinary time in their life.

Manufactured by Amazon.ca
Bolton, ON